THE TOMB OF

IOUIYA AND TOUIYOU.

PLATE I.

THE CHARIOT.

THEODORE M. DAVIS'
EXCAVATIONS: BIBÂN EL MOLÛK.

THE TOMB OF
IOUIYA AND TOUIYOU.

THE FINDING OF THE TOMB,

BY

THEODORE M. DAVIS.

NOTES ON IOUIYA AND TOUIYOU,

BY

GASTON MASPERO.

DESCRIPTION OF THE OBJECTS FOUND IN THE TOMB,

BY

PERCY E. NEWBERRY.

ILLUSTRATIONS OF THE OBJECTS,

BY

HOWARD CARTER.

Duckworth

The Tomb of Iouiya and Touiyou first published in 1907
The Funeral Papyrus of Iouiya first published in 1908
by Archibald Constable & Co. Ltd.
Reprinted in one volume in May 2000 by
Gerald Duckworth & Co. Ltd.
61 Frith Street, London W1V 5TA
Tel: 0207 434 4242
Fax: 0207 434 4420
Email: enquiries@duckworth-publishers.co.uk
www.ducknet.co.uk

Second impression June 2000

Foreword © 2000 by Nicholas Reeves

A catalogue record for this book is available
from the British Library

ISBN 0 7156 2963 8

Printed in Great Britain by Bath Press, Bath

CONTENTS.

FOREWORD

'For some moments we couldn't see anything much, but as our eyes got used to the candle light we saw a sight which I can safely say no living man has ever seen. The chamber was pretty large – a rough hewn cavern of a place. In the middle of the room were two enormous sarcophagi of wood inlaid with gold. The lids had been wrenched off by [ancient] plunderers and the coffins inside had been tumbled about so that the two mummies were exposed ... All round ... were chairs, tables, beds, vases ... [It] looked just as a drawing room would look in a London house shut up while the people were away for the summer. But with this terrifying difference – that everything was in the fashion of 34 centuries ago ...

'[Gaston] Maspero, [Theodore] Davis and I stood there gaping and almost trembling ...'

(Letter from Arthur Weigall to his wife Hortense, 14-16 February 1905, quoted in J. Hankey, 'Arthur Weigall and the tomb of Yuya and Thuyu', *KMT. A Modern Journal of Ancient Egypt*, vol. 9, no. 2, summer 1998, pp. 42-3)

Such were the powerful first impressions of archaeologist Arthur Weigall on entering the tomb of Yuya (Iouiya) and Tjuyu (Touiyou), penned in a letter home to his wife only a short time after the discovery in February 1905. As Weigall's wide-open eyes flitted from one glorious treasure to another, finally coming to rest on the fine, mummified features of the deceased and his wife, it was as if time had stood still. When Yuya and Tjuyu were laid to rest within their tomb, the thoughts of Christ and the prophet Mohammed were a millennium and more in the future; while during the years the mummies had gazed sightlessly up at the rock-cut roof of their burial chamber, the empires of Assyria and Persia, Greece and Rome had come, gone, and passed into distant history themselves.

Before the discovery of Tutankhamun, Yuya and Tjuyu's tomb was one of the most fabulous ever to have been uncovered, its contents perfect and of a richness and sophistication seldom encountered. The find spawned several publications, principal among which were Theodore Davis's *The Tomb of Iouiya and Touiyou* and its companion volume, *The Funeral Papyrus of Iouiya;* prepared in collaboration with the leading authorities of the day, they were illustrated by splendid photographic plates and a series of exquisite watercolours from the brush of Howard Carter. A third volume, *The Tomb of Yuaa and Thuiu,* was compiled by J.E. Quibell and published in 1908 in the Cairo Museum's Catalogue général series; while a recent reassessment of the find is in C.N. Reeves, *Valley of the Kings: the decline of a royal necropolis* (London, 1990), pp. 148-53, with notes on pp. 160-5.

Yuya and Tjuyu were no ordinary people: they were the father- and mother-in-law of pharaoh Amenophis III, 'the Magnificent', and great-grandparents of the boy-king Tutankhamun himself. As powers close to the throne, among the élite of the élite, Yuya and Tjuyu will have known and experienced much. Though their voices have fallen silent, they speak to us still through their favoured possessions and the magical paraphernalia assembled for their perilous translation from this world to the next.

London, January 2000   Nicholas Reeves

PREFACE.

I DESIRE to express my gratitude to Monsieur Maspero for writing the Notes on Iouiya and Touiyou.

THEODORE M. DAVIS.

NEWPORT,
    RHODE ISLAND,
        U.S.A.

LIST OF PLATES.

LIST OF ILLUSTRATIONS IN THE TEXT.

NOTICE ON IOUIYA AND TOUIYOU.

PLATE II.

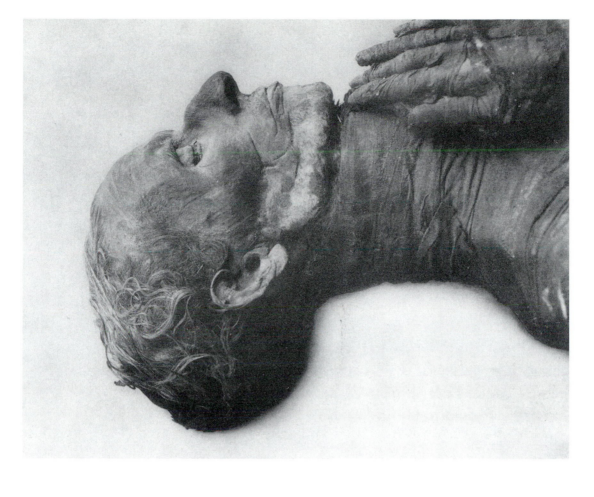

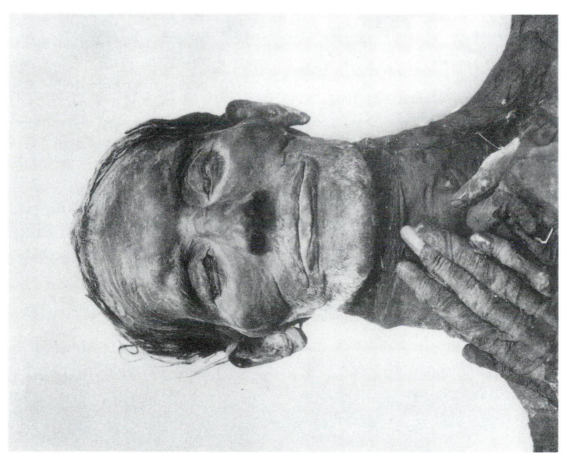

FULL FACE AND PROFILE OF THE MUMMY OF IOUIYA.

NOTICE ON IOUIYA AND TOUIYOU,

BY

G. MASPERO.

STRICTLY speaking, these two individuals are not in themselves historical characters : it is through their daughter Tîyi, wife of Amenôthes III and mother of Khouniatonou, that they attract the attention of modern historians of Egypt.

§ I.—NAMES AND TITLES OF THE TWO PERSONAGES.

The name of the wife is spelt consistently with the exception of a few differences in calligraphy usual at this period. It is written 𓎛𓇋𓍑𓏏, less frequently 𓎛𓇋𓍑, 𓎛𓇋𓍑𓏏, with or without the female determinative : the probable reading of it is *Touîyou*.

The man's name assumes several forms of spelling, which differ somewhat from each other : these are not all to be found on the same monument. It appears that each scribe or craftsman employed in the making of the funereal furniture had adopted his own rendering of the name for the objects that he decorated. On the black square sarcophagi and on the gilded coffins for the human remains the name is written 𓇋𓅿𓅿𓀭, and exceptionally 𓇋𓅿𓅿𓀭, with or without the determinative for the dead ; but one meets 𓇋𓇋𓅿𓇋𓅿 on the two small scent chests, and on the canopic boxes 𓇋𓅿𓇋𓅿, on the small *ouashbaatiou* [ushabti] coffin 𓇋𓇋𓅿𓇋𓅿𓀭, and rarely 𓇋𓅿𓇋𓇋𓀭, 𓇋𓇋𓇋𓅿, 𓇋𓅿𓇋𓇋, and 𓇋𓇋𓅿𓇋𓅿 on the *ouashbaatiou* (ushabti) themselves ; finally ⟨hieroglyphs⟩ on the remains of the gilded cartonage, and ⟨hieroglyphs⟩ on the small limestone vases capped by figures of animals. All these varieties group themselves around two chief forms, both dissyllabic, both beginning with ⟨hieroglyphs⟩ or with its variants ⟨hieroglyph⟩ and ⟨hieroglyphs⟩, once ⟨hieroglyph⟩, but where the sounds ⟨hieroglyph⟩ and ⟨hieroglyph⟩ interchange. To judge from the number of the variants, the most usual pronunciation would be ⟨hieroglyphs⟩ *Iouîa*, but it would be equally well pronounced ⟨hieroglyphs⟩ *Iaîou* by interchange of the vowels, and even ⟨hieroglyphs⟩ *Iaîya*. In names composed exclusively of vowels or semi-vowels, pronunciation has always a tendency to fluctuate more easily than in names that are full of consonants.

Of their titles, some denote real functions, others are those of courtesy. Collecting them together from the monuments throughout which they are scattered, the following groups are obtained :—

Firstly for the man, ⟨hieroglyphs⟩ or ⟨hieroglyphs⟩ or ⟨hieroglyphs⟩ ; ⟨hieroglyphs⟩ developed into ⟨hieroglyphs⟩, ⟨hieroglyphs⟩, ⟨hieroglyphs⟩, ⟨hieroglyphs⟩ ; ⟨hieroglyphs⟩ ; ⟨hieroglyphs⟩, with its variants ⟨hieroglyphs⟩ and ⟨hieroglyphs⟩, ⟨hieroglyph⟩, once ⟨hieroglyphs⟩ ; ⟨hieroglyphs⟩ ; ⟨hieroglyphs⟩ ; ⟨hieroglyphs⟩.

The above are the real titles of the dead. The first indicate his rank at court ⟨hieroglyphs⟩. *Rapâîti-haîti* classes him among the feudal nobility, whilst ⟨hieroglyphs⟩ *Nîtî? baîti* and ⟨hieroglyphs⟩ *Samirou* would accord to him in the ranks of the priesthood the position of "one attached to the Person of the king" (*Homme au collier du roi*) of Lower Egypt, and "friend"; the title of "friend" in the titulary of Upper Egypt appears to correspond with the title "one attached to the Person" in the titulary of Lower Egypt. The accompanying symbols which qualify the word ⟨hieroglyphs⟩ prove that he held an eminent place among the people of this class : he was in truth "the first friend of the friends" ⟨hieroglyphs⟩ *samîr tapou ne samirou*, and "first friend of those who love the king of Upper Egypt and of those who love the king of Lower Egypt" ⟨hieroglyphs⟩ *samir-tapou marourou souton, marourou baîti*, and then "unique friend of love" ⟨hieroglyphs⟩ *samîr uâou-ni-marouît*, or ⟨hieroglyphs⟩ *samîr âou-ni-marouît*. The second class of titles

PLATE III

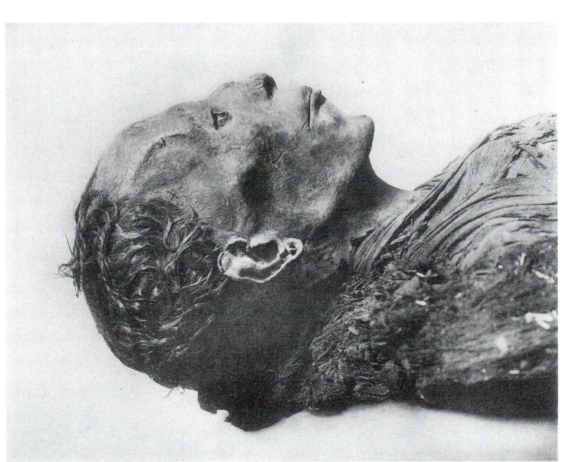

PROFILE AND FULL-FACE OF THE MUMMY OF TOUIYOU.

denote the active duties he fulfilled, and they show us that his services were of the priestly order. Two of them are only suggested in passing, and as if with reluctance, those of "the prophet of Mînou" *honnoutir ni Mînou*, and "the superintendent of the (sacred) oxen of Mînou, the lord of Akhmîm" *nas-ahaou ni Mînou nab Iapou*. His title of "master of the horse, lieutenant of the king for the chariots," comes only once, and seems to prove that he had been connected with the war-administration, not that he ever went to the wars. The one title to which he holds and which describes him is that of *iat-noutir*, or "divine father," of which the usual variants are *iatf-noutir* and , . One of these variants, *iatf-noutir ni nab taouî*, "the divine father of the gods of the two lands" (that is to say, the king), is important, as we shall have occasion to see.

After the titles proper come titles by courtesy, which are numerous. Iouîya is called *ouâou akirou*, "the one wise," and *sâaou ni souton saoukirou ni baîti iri ni nab-taou-ka-f*, which, translated, verbally means "he who is *le fait grand* of the king of Upper Egypt, *le fait sage* of the king of Lower Egypt," in French, "celui que le roi a rendu grand et sage" [he whom the king has made great and wise], "for whom the king has made his double." One variant gives *sâaou ni nab-iri-khaîtou*, with the title of "lord [or master] to do what pleases him" which belongs to the king. The most noteworthy series of these epithets includes the words *Hosou* and *marout*: *hosoui paroui me khaîtou hosouiou*, literally, "he whose praises are sung, coming out from the mass (lit., "from the body") of those whose praises are sung," or nearly, "the favourite excellent above all favourites," *hosoui ni noutir nofir*, "the favourite of the good god," *hosoui ni nab-taoui*, "the favourite of the lord of the two lands," *hosoui ni nabou-f*, "the favourite of his lord," *hosoui ni Horou mepaou-f*, "the favourite of the Horus in his palace." Most commonly the designation "lord" indicates the king, but in other cases it denotes a god, *hosoui ni nabou-f Amanou*, "the favourite of his lord Ammon," *Nab hosouîtou khar nab-taoui*, "the lord of favours under the lord of the two lands," [hieroglyphs] *didou-hosouîtou man marouît khar nabou-f Osiri*, literally, "the lasting of favours, the unchanging of love under his lord Osiris," [hieroglyphs] *man marouît khar nabou-f ashaou hosouîtou me par-souton*, that is to say, "he who rejoices in the unchanging love of his lord, and who has many favours in the Royal Palace"; in short, he is the [hieroglyphs] *mah-iabou ni noutir noufir*, "he who fills the heart of the good god" and [hieroglyphs] *maroui nabou-f*, "he who loves his lord," [hieroglyphs] *mah-iabou ni souton me ta-re-zarou-f*, "he who fills the heart of the king in the whole land," with other ordinary expressions which are used in reference to all people of high rank, [hieroglyphs] *ouâou iabou ni souton ane mah-snaou-f*, "the unique beloved of the king, without a second," [hieroglyphs] *âm-iabou ni noutir nofir*, "he who is in the heart of the good god," [hieroglyphs] *ra-ni-souton ânkhoui-nou-baîti*, "the mouth of the southern king, the two ears of the northern king," and so on. The whole extent of his favour is summed up in the expressive sentence: [hieroglyphs] *rapaîti haîti nasou tenou ounouît re shapou hosouîtou nabou-taoui*, "the prince who is called at any hour to receive the praises (lit. 'the songs') of the lord of both lands." His coffin was [hieroglyphs] *iroui me hosonîtou nit khir souton*, "made by the special favour of the king."

For the wife the titles and formulæ are less varied than for the man. It is apparent that in the beginning her real duties were at court in her capacity of [hieroglyphs] *khakerouît souten*, "dresser to the king," and at the temple of [hieroglyphs] *qamaît ni Amanou*, "chantress of Amon," and of [hieroglyphs] *ouarît khonaî nit Amanou*, with the variant [hieroglyphs] *ouarît khonaît ni Amanou*, "lady of the harem of Amon"; just as her husband was attached to the cult of Mînou of Panopolis, as we have already seen above, she held in relation to that god the same position as she held to Amon, [hieroglyphs] *ouarît khonaît ni Mînou*, "lady of the harem of Minou." Her customary attribute in her capacity of "dresser to the king" is [hieroglyphs] *hosouît nit noutir nofir*, "favourite of the good god," with the purely grammatical variants [hieroglyphs] *hosoui nit noutir nofir*, and of [hieroglyphs] *hosouît ni noutir nofir.* Sometimes, however, she is called 𓀭𓇌𓇌𓂋𓄿 *hosouît ni Hathor,* "the favoured of Hathor." Always her principal title, that of which she was most proud, and which brought her chiefly before the notice of her contemporaries, is that of 𓀭𓂋𓅃𓏏𓏤𓇓, variant 𓀭𓅃𓏏𓏤𓇓, *maout souton ni himît souton ouarît,* "royal mother of the chief-wife of the king." This is repeated jealously on the coffins, on the furniture, on the *ouashbaatiou* [ushabti figures], in such a manner that the day an intruder should penetrate into the tomb, he would know from what to refrain on account of the quality of one of the persons resting there, and would not be able to plead the excuse of ignorance if he persisted in his intention of despoiling the mummy.

To sum up, Iouîya and Touîyou possessed a double set of titles, corresponding to the two successive conditions of their career. At their outset they are people of mediocre position. The one, Iouîya, is "divine father," that is to say, if the title is a priestly title, he occupied one of the least important positions in the priestly order, one which was bestowed upon children; the other, Touîyou, fills a position which brings her into relations with the sovereign, that of "dresser" [mistress of the robes] 𓆟, and she is, like all the ladies who attended the court, "chantress of Amon." Perhaps the titles that belong to them in the priesthood and administration of the god Mînou of Panopolis show to us that the two conjointly, or at least the more important of the two, namely, Iouîya, originally came from Akhmîm.

There is, perhaps, reason to think that the post occupied at court by Touîyou facilitated the marriage of her daughter with the sovereign. The daughter came to the palace, where she would reside with her mother, supposing the latter to have had apartments therein, as it is possible, considering her position; it is there that Amenôthes III, or, if the marriage was arranged by the regent-mother of Amenôthes III, that the former was able to see the young girl. It has happened more than once in Oriental harems that a woman of no particular position, or a simple slave, devoted to the amusement of a young prince whilst waiting the opportunity for a suitable marriage, has gained so great a hold upon her young master that she has got herself espoused and become queen. What we now know of the parents of Tîyi and of their circumstances, allows us to conjecture some such adventure. The Pharaoh, in making their daughter his wife, loaded them with favours, and heaped on them the second mass of titles of which I have spoken: there it was that Iouîya became *divine father of the lord of both lands,* if the title must really, as Borchardt has given very good reasons to believe, be interpreted in such cases *father-in-law of the king*.[1] For the rest, we do not see that they played any part in State affairs : they remained the private parents of a queen, and were never otherwise.

§ II.—THE CHILDREN.

Touîyou had two children, or at least we know the names of two of her children, the only ones perhaps who lived to grow up : a son whose existence has been proved to us by the legends on her sarcophagus and on her coffin, 𓀀𓏥𓏏... *Sai-s honnoutir mah-snaou ni Amanou hosouî ni noutir nofir Aanenou,* "the second prophet of Amon, the favourite of the good god Aanenou." The daughter became the Queen Tîyi 𓇋𓇋, the favourite of Amenôthes III and the mother of Amenôthes IV Khouniatonou. None of the inscriptions found in the tomb say that Tîyi was the daughter of Iouîya, and one would be able to suppose that she was born of a previous marriage of Touîyou, if the legends on the large scarabs of Amenôthes III did not definitely state that she had as father Iouîya 𓏏𓅱𓀀.

For the last half-century many efforts have been made to prove that Queen Tîyi was not of Egyptian extraction, but Asiatic, in consequence of her father and mother being Syrians, whether private individuals or princes. Without dwelling upon more remote work, I will quote what has been written upon this subject by Petrie and Budge in their histories of Egypt. Petrie comes to the conclusion from the facial type of Tîyi upon the monuments and the resemblance which she bears to one of the Asiatic prisoners at Karnak, "that she belonged to Northern Syria." He declares that the name of her parents may equally well be Egyptian as foreign, but from the character of the titles which she bears, he concludes she was an hereditary princess of blood royal. "She could have easily been grand-"daughter of an Egyptian king and queen, her mother Thuaa having been "married to some North Syrian prince Yuaa. Thus she would have the

[1] L. Borchardt, *der ægyptische Titel " Vater des Gottes " als Bezeichnung für " Vater oder Schwiegervater des Kœnigs,"* extract from the *Berichte der K. Sächsischen Gesellschaft der Wissenschaften zu Leipzig,* LVII. pp. 256–270.

" right to be a 'princess of both lands;' her name might be Egyptian; and
" she would rightfully fill the prominent place she did in Egypt; while her
" physiognomy would be Syrian. This view cannot be yet proved, but it
" certainly fulfils all the conditions closely."[1]

Budge, on his side, assures us that " of all the Mesopotamian or North
" Syrian women whom Amen-hetep married, the best beloved was the
" beautiful Thi, or Tii . . . . None of the other Asiatic wives was
" acknowledged to be 'Queen of Egypt,' this honour being reserved solely
" for the lady Thi . . . . : she·seems not to have belonged to any royal
" house in Mesopotamia, but it is perfectly certain that she was accorded the
" highest rank and honour which a woman could obtain in Egypt, when she
" is described as 'royal daughter, royal sister, royal mother, royal wife, great
" lady, lady of the South and North.' The lady with whom she is identified
" is represented as having a fair complexion and blue eyes, and she has all
" the physical characteristics of the women belonging to certain families who
" may be seen in North-Eastern Syria to this day."[2]

It is interesting to look into the reasons that moved the Egyptologists of
the last generation to believe and attempt to prove that queen Tîyi was a
foreigner. Some are of moral sort, others material. Struck, in fact, by the
influence she exercised over her son Amenôthes IV, and by the part which
she seemed to take in the ritual of the cult of Atonou, they questioned if it
was not owing to her that this cult came into such sudden favour. Just as
Atonou has the ring of the names of the Semitic divinities Adonaî, Adonis,
they concluded that Atonou was a Semitic god, in consequence of the queen
being a Semite, or at least of Syrian extraction. In searching for proofs of
the above hypothesis, they found them clad in a shroud of facts, or rather
conjectures, which they arranged for themselves skilfully. There was in the
" Bab el-Harim " the tomb of a queen whose name 𓈖 Taîti, transcribed into
modern languages, presented a remote similarity with that of 𓇋𓇋𓏏 Tîyi:
these they identified with each other, and all that is attributed to the second
they attributed to the first. Again, in 1893, Mr. Budge showed that " the
" tomb of a queen Thi, who is designated royal daughter, royal sister, royal
" wife, chief lady, regent of the North and South,[3] was opened at the beginning
" of this century at Thebes. It would hardly be possible to doubt that this

[1] Petrie, *A History of Egypt*, 3rd edit., Vol. II, pp. 182, 183.
[2] Budge, *A History of Egypt*, Vol. IV, pp. 96–98.
[3] Brugsch, *Recueil de Monuments Égyptiens*, Vol. II, Pl. LXIII, i.

3.

"was the tomb of the principal wife of Amenophis III. The portrait of this "lady [1] represents her with a fair complexion and blue eyes; the colour of "the skin is that of the complexion of the original people of the north-east of "Syria. Thi was the mother of Amenophis IV. She also gave birth to a "daughter Set-Amen.[2] The British Museum possesses a kohl pot of blue "faïence [3] and a double case for kohl in wood [4] with the name of Amenophis "and of Thi. They formed, probably, part of the toilet requisites deposited "in the tomb for the use of the queen." [5] The identification was a mistake, and the queen buried at Bab el-Harim had nothing in common with Tîyi, not even the name; she was called Taîtï $\bigwedge_{\shortmid\shortmid}^{\frown}$, as I have said before, and she lived during the XXth dynasty, as is proved by the character of her tomb.

The points brought forward to give proof of her Asiatic origin do not exist, or prove nothing. She has not blue eyes, as is ordinarily stated: the drawing by Rosellini, to which one refers for detail, gives her dark eyes, and the blue eyes which one sees in *l'Histoire de l'Art Égyptien* are a restoration by Prisse d'Avennes, which nothing that is to be seen on the monuments justifies. As to the white, or rather pink, hue with which the skin of Taîti is coloured, I have already had occasion to point out by numerous examples that this was the fashion at many times during the Theban period: the men and women painted themselves in this manner to lighten the colour of their skin, and it would be wrong to see a suggestion of origin in what was merely a caprice of fashion. The identification of Taîti with Tîyi cannot be upheld a moment when the original documents have been resorted to; but the mistake by which this had been produced, and the false conclusions drawn from it, once it was scattered through the world of scholars and intelligent readers, could no more be destroyed. Assyriologists in particular are attached to this theory with still greater persistency perhaps than Egyptologists, and it is they above all who have insisted that Tîyi was daughter and sister of the kings of Mitanni. The chief reason they bring forward is that these princes call her "their sister;" but the terms "brother" and "sister" already formed part of the international courtesies at this distant epoch, and no more than now in such a case would

---

[1] Rosellini, *Monumenti Storici*, Pl. XIX, No. 22.

[2] This is proved by an inscription engraved on a piece of wood in the British Museum, No. 5899a.

[3] No. 2572b, Fourth Egyptian Hall, North Gallery, Case E.

[4] No. 2598a, Fourth Egyptian Hall, Case E.

[5] Bezold–Budge, *The Tell el-Amarna Tablets in the British Museum*, pp. xix, xx.

it imply family relationship. Everything considered, the hypothesis of Syrian origin for Queen Tîyi rests upon a collection of mistaken theories and of badly interpreted facts ; and as she herself was the only valid reason for making Iouîya and Touîyou foreigners, the desire to make them other than Egyptian must be renounced at once. Equally their titles connect them with Egyptian sacred rites. Their names have not the form of Mitanni names as Doushratta, Tadoukhipa, Giloukhipa, but they resemble Libyan names so frequent in Egypt.

The racial type of the woman is like enough that of the queen Tîyi according to the statues, and it is certain that she very closely resembled her mother ; notwithstanding that, she possesses some of the firmness noticeable in her father. As to deciding from these particulars whether her parents were of African or Asiatic race, I will not hazard an opinion ; nothing is less certain than ethnographical conclusions drawn from the examination of bas-reliefs when it is not concerned with races as different in type as black from white. A people like that of the Egyptians contained in themselves every variety of type possible, whether these types spring naturally and without mixing from the original type, whether they result from alliances more or less remote with individuals belonging to a foreign unmixed race, or to the Egyptian race contaminated more or less by foreign elements. The profile of the queen Tîyi recalls to Mr. Petrie that of a Syrian prisoner. The head of a statuette of this same queen discovered at Sinai during the winter of 1905, recalls to me the impression of women of the Ababdehs and Begas whom I have seen at Assuan ; I could thus assign to Iouîya a Nubian origin. When criticism is so undecided, the best is to abstain and to reserve judgment. Until we have new evidence, I shall consider that Iouîya, Touîyou, and Tîyi as being natives of the country wherein they lived and where their mummies have been found.

§ III.—THEIR AGE.

Iouîya and Touîyou died at a fairly advanced age : their hairs are white, and the examination of their bodies does not contradict the verdict of their hair. It will not be a mistake to state that they had reached an age over sixty. From the relative position of the two sarcophagi in the tomb, it seems that the husband was the first to die ; but the material is lacking to decide this question.

THE FINDING OF THE TOMB OF IOUIYA AND TOUIYOU.

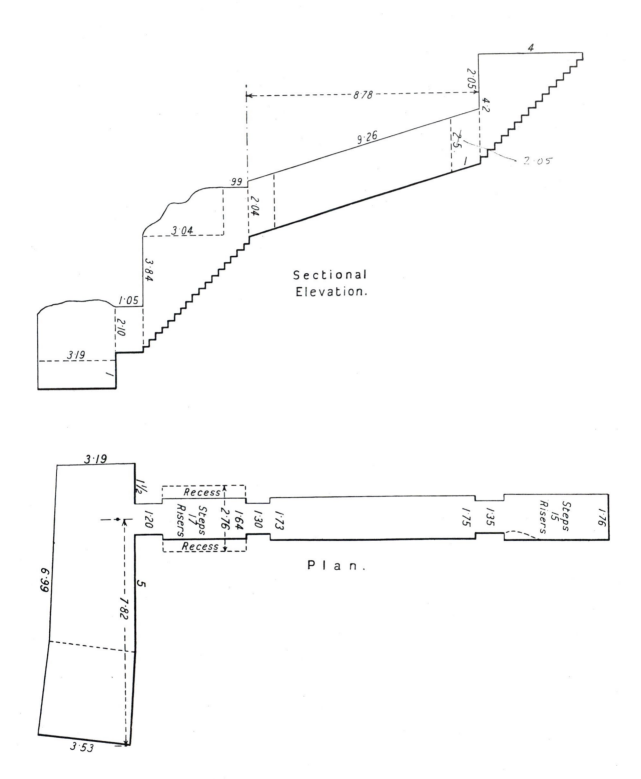

Sectional Elevation.

Plan.

PLAN AND SECTIONAL ELEVATION OF THE TOMB.

PLATE IV.

ENTRANCE TO THE TOMB.

THE FINDING OF THE TOMB OF IOUIYA AND TOUIYOU.

In the "Valley of the Kings," on the west side of the Nile at Thebes, there is a narrow lateral valley, nearly half a mile long, leading up to the mountain. At the mouth of this valley there is a foothill about sixty feet high, in the side of which Ramses III commenced a tomb, and beyond which Ramses XII excavated his tomb. In the winters of 1902 and 1903 I undertook to clear and explore this valley, commencing just above the tomb of Ramses XII, and continuing my work until I reached the mountain. It resulted in the discovery of the tombs of Thoutmôsis IV and of Queen Hâtshopsîtû.

On the 20th of December, 1904, I resumed my explorations in the lower end of the lateral valley, which I was enabled to do owing to the kindness of Mr. J. E. Quibell, the Chief Inspector at Thebes, who, with the approval of Monsieur Maspero, Director-General of the Cairo Museum, undertook the employment and superintendence of my workmen, pending my arrival in the valley.

On my arrival in January, 1905, I found that the work on the location selected had yielded nothing and gave no promise. Consequently I abandoned the site, and transferred my workmen to the unexplored space between the tombs of Ramses III and Ramses XII, heretofore described.

The site was most unpromising, lying as it did between the Ramses tombs, which had required many men for many years; therefore it did not seem possible that a tomb could have existed in so narrow a space without being discovered. As an original proposition I would not have explored it, and certainly no Egyptologist, exploring with another person's money, would have thought of risking the time and expense. But I knew every yard of the lateral valley, except the space described, and I decided that good exploration justified its investigation, and that it would be a satisfaction to know the entire valley, even if it yielded nothing.

4

From the 25th of January, 1905, until the 5th of February, the work progressed without sign of promise. My daily visits were most discouraging, but on my arrival at the work on the 6th February, I was greeted by my Reis (Captain) and workmen with great acclamation. I quickly made my way to the spot, where I saw a few inches of the top of a well-cut stone step, which promised steps below and the possible existence of a tomb.

From the 6th of February until the 11th my workmen were hard at work removing the overhanging *débris* which concealed the door; but before the night of the 11th a small portion of the doorway was exposed, and from that moment the opening was guarded day and night by policemen and valley guards. At the close of the twelfth day the door was entirely cleared—a most satisfactory sight! It was cut in the solid rock, and was 4·02 metres high and 1·35 wide, with a decorated lintel. The doorway was closed within eighteen inches of the top with flat stones, about twelve inches by four, laid in Nile mud plaster. This opening clearly indicated that, at some early date, the tomb had been entered and probably robbed—a most unwelcome indication! Although it was nearly dark, I concluded to have a look through the opening. Mr. Arthur Weigall, the appointed but not formally confirmed Chief Inspector in succession to Mr. Quibell, had ridden out to the valley with me, and was invited to join me in the first sight of the corridor of the tomb. The opening was chin high, but we could dimly see a few yards of the corridor, which seemed to be about five feet wide and high, with a steep decline. As soon as my eyes became used to the semi-darkness, I saw what I thought to be a cane, or small club, lying on the floor a few feet from the doorway. Neither of us could get up to the opening, nor through it, without a ladder—which did not exist in the valley— so I selected a small native boy and had him lifted up to the opening, through which he entered. We watched the boy closely and saw him pick up the cane; then he came towards us, picked up two other objects and passed them to me. They proved to be a wooden staff of office, a neck yoke, and a large stone scarab, covered more or less with gold-foil, which made it seem, at first glance, to be solid gold.

Happily, Monsieur Maspero was on his dahabeah at Luxor, and, as soon as I reached mine, I wrote him a note asking him to come over and see something worth looking at. Shortly thereafter he came, followed by Professor Sayce, and we not only enjoyed the discoveries of the day, but were even more interested in the ownership of the tomb, as to which we had not the slightest clue. Monsieur Maspero requested me to open and enter

PLATE V.

POTTERY BOWLS FOUND ON EITHER SIDE OF THE DOOR TO THE INNER CHAMBER.

the tomb next day, that he might show it to H.R.H. the Duke of Connaught and party, who were expected to arrive on the following afternoon.

Consequently, next morning, Monsieur Maspero and Mr. Weigall joined me at the tomb, and I at once set the men to work taking down the wall which barred the outer door. It was very slow work, as every stone had to be examined for hieroglyphs and signs, and every basket of sand and *débris* sifted and examined for objects of interest which might be concealed in the deposit. However, nothing was found, and, in the course of an hour or so, the doorway was cleared.

The electric wire had been installed at the outer doorway, but as the introduction down the corridor would have required the services of electricians, we concluded that it would be safer to use candles for our entry and examinations. Monsieur Maspero and I and, at my invitation, Mr. Weigall, each with a candle, started down the corridor, which proved to be 1·75 metres wide and 2·05 metres high, cut out of the solid rock and descending so sharply as to require care not to fall. It was neither painted nor inscribed. After descending about twenty feet, we found a shelf cut into one side of the wall and on it a large ceremonial wig made of flax and dyed black, also an armful of dried flowers which doubtless were offerings to the dead (as is done in our day and generation). Passing on some 9 metres, we came to another flight of stone steps descending almost perpendicularly, at the bottom of which we found a doorway 2·10 metres high and 1·20 metres wide, closed with stones set in Nile mud plaster, with an opening at the top of about the same size as was found in the first doorway, confirming our fears of a robbery. The face of the wall was plastered with mud and stamped from top to bottom with seals.

On either side of this doorway, carefully placed to escape injury, stood a reddish pottery bowl about twelve inches wide, showing the finger-marks of the man who with his hands gathered the mud and plastered it on the doorway wall. In each bowl was a wide wooden stick, evidently used to scrape the mud from his hands. Having copied the seals, we investigated the possibility of entry without taking down the wall. We found that the opening which the robber had made was too high and too small to allow of Monsieur Maspero getting through without injury. Though we had nothing but our bare hands, we managed to take down the upper layer of stones, and then Monsieur Maspero and I put our heads and candles into the chamber, which enabled us to get a glimpse of shining gold covering some kind of furniture, though we could not identify it. This stimulated us to

4.

make the entry without further enlarging the opening. I managed to get over the wall and found myself in the sepulchral chamber. With considerable difficulty we helped Monsieur Maspero safely to scale the obstruction, and then Mr. Weigall made his entry. The chamber was as dark as dark could be and extremely hot. Our first quest was the name of the owner of the tomb, as to which we had not the slightest knowledge or suspicion. We held up our candles, but they gave so little light and so dazzled our eyes that we could see nothing except the glitter of gold. In a moment or two, however, I made out a very large wooden coffin, known as a funeral sled, which was used to contain all the coffins of the dead person and his mummy and to convey them to his tomb. It was about six feet high and eight feet long, made of wood covered with bitumen, which was as bright as the day it was put on. Around the upper part of the coffin was a stripe of gold-foil, about six inches wide, covered with hieroglyphs. On calling Monsieur Maspero's attention to it, he immediately handed me his candle, which, together with my own, I held before my eyes, close to the inscriptions so that he could read them. In an instant he said, "Iouiya." Naturally excited by the announcement, and blinded by the glare of the candles, I involuntarily advanced them very near the coffin; whereupon Monsieur Maspero cried out, "Be careful!" and pulled my hands back. In a moment we realized that, had my candles touched the bitumen, which I came dangerously near doing, the coffin would have been in a blaze. As the entire contents of the tomb were inflammable, and directly opposite the coffin was a corridor leading to the open air and making a draught, we undoubtedly should have lost our lives, as the only escape was by the corridor, which would have necessitated climbing over the stone wall barring the doorway. This would have retarded our exit for at least ten minutes.

As soon as we realised the danger we had escaped, we made our way out of the chamber and, seating ourselves in the corridor, sent for workmen, who took down the door blocking the doorway. . Then the electricians brought down the wires with bulbs attached, and we made our second entry into the chamber, each of us furnished with electric lights which we held over our heads, and we saw that every foot of the chamber was filled with objects brilliant with gold. In a corner stood a chariot, the pole of which had been broken by the weight of a coffin lid that the robber had evidently deposited upon it. Within a foot or two of the chariot stood two alabaster vases of great beauty and in perfect condition.

From the neck of one of the vases hung shreds of mummy-cloth which had originally covered the mouth of the vase. Evidently the robber, expecting the contents to be valuable, tore off the cloth. Three thousand years thereafter I looked into the vase with like expectation ; both of us were disappointed, for it contained only a liquid which was first thought to be honey, but which subsequently proved to be natron.

The mummies of Iouiya and Touiyou were lying in their coffins. Originally each mummy was enclosed in three coffins ; the inner one holding the body. Evidently the robber had taken the inner coffins out and then had taken off their lids, though he did not take the bodies out of their coffins, but contented himself with stripping off the mummy-cloth in which they were wrapped. The stripping was done by scratching off the cloth with his nails, seeking only the gold ornaments or jewels. At least that seems to have been the manner of robbing the bodies, as we found in both coffins, on either side of the bodies, great quantities of mummy-cloth torn into small bits. Among the shreds were found numerous valuable religious symbols, several scarabs, and various objects of interest and beauty. In lifting the body of Iouiya from his coffin, we found a necklace of large beads made of gold and of lapis lazuli, strung on a strong thread, which the robber had evidently broken when scratching off the mummy-cloth, causing the beads to fall behind the mummy's neck.

The robber had also overlooked a gold plate about the size of the palm of a man's hand, which had been inserted by the embalmer to conceal the incision he had made in extracting the dead man's heart for special mummification.

When I first saw the mummy of Touiyou she was lying in her coffin, covered from her chin to her feet with very fine mummy-cloth arranged with care. Why this was done no one can positively state, but I am disposed to think that the robber was impressed by the dignity of the dead woman whose body he had desecrated. I had occasion to sit by her in the tomb for nearly an hour, and having nothing else to do or see, I studied her face and indulged in speculations germane to the situation, until her dignity and character so impressed me that I almost found it necessary to apologize for my presence.

From all the evidence furnished by the acts of the robber, it seems reasonable to conclude that the entry into the tomb was made within the lifetime of some person who had exact knowledge of its location. Evidently the robber had tunnelled through the overlying *débris* which concealed the door of the tomb ; otherwise he would have been compelled to remove a mass of rock and soil which would have required many days, and would also have exposed the robbery to the first passer-by. When the robber found the outer doorway barred by a wall, he took off enough of it to enable him to crawl through ; and when he reached the second and last doorway, he found a corresponding wall, which he treated in the same manner. He seems to have had either a very dim light or none at all, for when he was in the burial chamber he selected a large stone scarab, the neck-yoke of the chariot, and a wooden staff of office, all of which were covered with thick gold foil, which evidently he thought to be solid gold : he carried them up the corridor until he came to a gleam of daylight, when he discovered his error and left them on the floor of the corridor, where I found them.

When the robber got out of the tomb, he carefully concealed the doorway and his tunnel with stones and *débris*, and did it so effectively, that it was not disturbed until its discovery three thousand years later.

The tomb which I have attempted to describe is the only one ever found which has contained in perfect condition the original deposit. It is sad to realize that thousands of kindred objects, probably more beautiful and instructive than the present find, have existed in tombs which in past years were robbed and their precious contents destroyed or scattered over the face of the world.

Though, under the letter of my permission to explore in the " Valley of the Kings," I was not entitled to any portion of the " find," Monsieur Maspero, with a generosity common to him, offered me a share. I confess that it was a most attractive offer, but, on consideration, I could not bring myself to break up the collection which I felt ought to be exhibited intact in the Cairo Museum, where it could be seen and studied by probably the greatest number of appreciative visitors.

THEODORE M. DAVIS.

DESCRIPTIONS OF THE OBJECTS

FOUND IN THE

TOMB OF IOUIYA AND TOUIYOU.

THE SARCOPHAGUS OF IOUIYA.

THE mummy of Iouiya was enclosed in three separate coffins, nested one within the other. These again were placed in a large rectangular wooden sarcophagus, the latter being mounted on a sledge with roller in front.

The sledge and sarcophagus are both of a coarse-grained wood covered with pitch and decorated with figures and hieroglyphic legends in stucco-gilt. In shape the sarcophagus is rectangular with a projecting curved cornice around the top; its lid is rounded on either side of a flat beam running down the axis, and has massive uprights at each end. The joints are mortice- and tenon-pinned and the roller is dovetailed into the frame of the sledge.

Down the central beam of the lid is a band of gold-foil with a hieroglyphic inscription in slight relief :—

On either side of this central band of hieroglyphs are four vertical lines of inscription which are continued down the sides of the sarcophagus : these inscriptions give prayers to the gods of the West for the deceased and recount Iouiya's various titles. Between these vertical lines of hieroglyphs, on both sides of the box, is a procession of gods : Thoth, Amset, Hapy, and Anubis. At the top end of the right-hand side is figured a pylon with the double eyes above it. The inscriptions read :—

On the right-hand side :—

(1)

(2)

5

(3) [hieroglyphic inscription]

(4) [hieroglyphic inscription]

On the left-hand side :—

(1) [hieroglyphic inscription]

(2) [hieroglyphic inscription]

(3) [hieroglyphic inscription]

(4) [hieroglyphic inscription]

On the two ends of the lid are, in low relief, figures of Anubis seated on pylons facing one another.

Immediately beneath the beading which separates the cornice from the rest of the box and running right round it is a band of gold with hieroglyphic inscriptions in slight relief. On the two ends are figures of Isis and Nephthys (in gold-foil) standing on *nub*-signs and reciting the incantations for the protection of the dead which are given in the inscriptions above them.

These inscriptions read :—

On the head of the box, above the figure of Isis :—

[hieroglyphic inscription]

On the end, above the figure of Nephthys :—

[hieroglyphic inscription]

On the right side of the box is a prayer to Unnefer for the benefit of the *ka* of Iouiya :

[hieroglyphic text]

On the left side of the box is a prayer to Osiris Khent-Amenti for the benefit of the *ka* of Iouiya :—

[hieroglyphic text]

OUTER COFFIN OF IOUIYA.

THE outer coffin is mummiform in shape, and, like the sarcophagus, is covered with pitch and ornamented with inscriptions and designs in stucco-gilt. The face and hands are gilt; the wig is long and the hair is represented by stripes of alternate black and gold. The eyes and eyebrows are inlaid: the eyebrows and lashes are of dark blue glass, the iris is of black obsidian and the white of white marble. Around the neck and upper part of the chest is a broad necklace in gold, and on the wrists are bracelets. Upon the abdomen is a vulture with outspread wings and holding the ○-rings in its talons. Down the front of the mummy case is a vertical line of hieroglyphs giving the title and name of Iouiya and the usual prayer to Nut :—

On either side of this central band of hieroglyphs are four vertical columns representing the mummy straps and inscribed with the titles and name of Iouiya. Between these vertical columns of hieroglyphs on both sides of the box is a procession of gods of the West, those on the right side being Mestha, Anubis, Duamutef and Geb; while on the left side are Hapŷ, Anubis, Qebhsenuf, and Nut. The inscriptions read :—

On the right :—

(1)   Iouiya.

(2)   Iouiya.

(3)   Iouiya.

(4)   Iouiya.

On the left :—

(1) [hieroglyphs] Iouiya.

(2) [hieroglyphs] Iouiya.

(3) [hieroglyphs] Iouiya.

(4) [hieroglyphs] Iouiya.

At the top end of the box on the right-hand side is figured a pylon with the double eyes above it, while on the left-hand side are two vertical lines of inscription stating that the coffin was made by favour of the king for Iouiya :—

(1) [hieroglyphs]   (2) [hieroglyphs]

Running round the head, sides and feet of the lid of the coffin is a band of gold-foil with four inscriptions. On the head of the box is a figure of Nephthys kneeling upon a *nub*-sign, and on the feet a figure of Isis also kneeling upon a *nub*-sign. The inscriptions round the lid give incantations for the protection of the dead, and read :—

(1) Round the head : [hieroglyphs]

[hieroglyphs]

(2) On the feet : [hieroglyphs]

(3) On the right side of the body : [hieroglyphs]

[hieroglyphs]

(4) On the left side of the body : [hieroglyphs]

[hieroglyphs]

SECOND COFFIN OF IOUIYA.

_____

THE second coffin, which is mummiform in shape, is of wood, coated with stucco and gold- and silver-foil, and richly inlaid with glass of various colours. The wig is long and the hair is represented by alternate bands of silver and gold. The face is gilt; the eyebrows and lashes are of blue glass inlaid, and the eyes are of white marble and obsidian. The necklace or pectoral is of gold inlaid with coloured glasses : its ends are the usual hawk heads, and it is composed of rows of poppy buds in red glass, petals of lotus flowers in dark blue glass and five bands of dark blue, light blue, and red glass. The hands are of gold-foil and project from the mummy wrappings : in the right hand is a 𓊽 amulet; in the left a 𓎬. On the wrists are bracelets of coloured glass inlaid. Over the abdomen is a vulture in gold inlaid in coloured glass with wings outspread and holding in its talons ⌖-seals of carnelian : above it are the signs 𓎼𓎶. Below the vulture is the goddess Nut standing upon a *nub*-sign and with arms upraised.

Around the coffin are figured the mummy-straps : two running vertically down each side of the goddess Nut, and four at equal spaces round the front and sides of the figure. The line on the right side of Nut gives the *De hetep seten* formula to Osiris that he may give the sweet breath of the north wind and oblations of wine and milk for the *ka* of Iouiya :—

On the left side the inscription gives the name and titles of Iouiya and the usual prayer to Nut.

The bands running round the front and sides of the case name the gods of the West, and give the following titles of Iouiya :—

On the right side of the coffin, on the box, is figured a procession of gods led by Thoth, with vertical lines of hieroglyphs between each figure. Before Thoth are two lines reading : (1) [hieroglyphs] (2) [hieroglyphs] Iouiya.

Then follow in order, Mestha : (1) [hieroglyphs] Iouiya (2) [hieroglyphs] (3) [hieroglyphs]

Anubis : (1) [hieroglyphs] (2) [hieroglyphs] Iouiya.

Duamut-ef : (1) [hieroglyphs] (2) [hieroglyphs] Iouiya [hieroglyphs] (3) [hieroglyphs]

Thoth : (1) [hieroglyphs] (2) [hieroglyphs] Iouiya.

On the left side of the coffin, on the box, is figured another procession of gods led by Thoth, and before him are the sacred eyes on a pylon and four vertical lines of hieroglyphs: (1) [hieroglyphs] (2) [hieroglyphs]
(3) [hieroglyphs] (4) [hieroglyphs]

Then follow in order, Hapŷ, with three vertical lines of inscription before him: (1) [hieroglyphs] (2) [hieroglyphs] [hieroglyphs] (3) [hieroglyphs]

Anubis: (1) [hieroglyphs] (2) [hieroglyphs] [hieroglyphs] (3) [hieroglyphs]

Kebhsenuef: (1) [hieroglyphs] (2) *sic* [hieroglyphs] [hieroglyphs] (3) [hieroglyphs] [hieroglyphs] *sic* [hieroglyphs]

Thoth: (1) [hieroglyphs] (2) [hieroglyphs] [hieroglyphs]

Round the bottom of the lid runs a band from head to foot upon which are three inscriptions inscribed horizontally: these are the same as those round the head and sides of the outer coffin with only unimportant variants.

On the lid at the feet is a figure of Isis with arms upraised and kneeling upon a *nub*-sign. Below her on the box are represented a *ded* and two *sa* amulets each inscribed with its chapter from the *Book of the Dead* (Chapters CLV and CLVI).

INNER COFFIN OF IOUIYA.

LIKE the second coffin of Iouiya, the third or inner one is mummiform in shape; it is carved in wood, coated with stucco and gilt, and richly inlaid with semi-precious stones and coloured glass. The wig is long; the face and ears are exquisitely modelled; the eyebrows and lashes are of blue glass inlaid, and the eyes are of white marble and black obsidian. The necklace or pectoral is of gold inlaid with coloured glasses: its ends are the usual hawk-heads, and it is composed of rows of beads and pendants in the form of poppy and lotus petals inlaid in red, and light and dark blue glass.

Over the abdomen is a vulture in gold inlaid with coloured glasses, with wings outspread, and holding in its talons ☉-seals of carnelian. Below it, covering the lower part of the abdomen and legs as far as the shins, is a standing figure of the goddess Nut in low relief, with arms upraised, and clad in a long close-fitting garment covered with bead work. She wears a long wig secured by a fillet over the forehead, a broad necklace, as well as bracelets and anklets. She stands upon a *nub*-sign.

On either side of the figure of Nut are vertical columns of hieroglyphs inlaid in coloured glasses. That on the right side gives the usual *de hetep seten* formula to Osiris Within the West, that he may give *per kheru* offerings for the benefit of the *ka* of Iouiya. On the left side the inscription gives the speech of Iouiya to Nut that she may spread her protecting wings over his body.

On the sides of the body are given in low relief the same inscriptions as are found on the second coffin, with figures of the Ibis-headed god Thoth at each end, and the gods of the West in the divisions between.

At the foot of the coffin is represented a figure of the goddess Isis kneeling upon a *nub*-sign. It is doubtful whether this case was originally made for Iouiya: another name seems to have been given on the sides, and that of Iouiya inserted over it.

MASK AND MUMMY-STRAPS OF IOUIYA.

MASK of Iouiya for fitting over the head of his mummy. It is made of several layers of coarse linen, glued together and coated with plaster. The inside is bitumened, the exterior is gilt. The wig is long, lined, and with bands at the ends. The face is finely modelled. The eyes, eyebrows and eyelashes are inlaid : the eyes are of white marble and obsidian, the eyelashes and brows are of blue glass. The pectoral consists of eleven bands of ornamental rectangles incised, with a row of drop-beads incised below. The chin and right side of the head are broken.

Fixed over the mummy wrappings of Iouiya were mummy-straps firmly secured by string behind. These are cut out of a piece of linen which forms their frame-work, and this is covered with stucco and gilt, with the margin painted green.

At the top is a figure of Nut with wings outspread, and on either side of her the amulets ⌗ and ⌗. The band running vertically down the chest gives the name and titles of Iouiya ⌗⌗⌗⌗⌗⌗⌗⌗⌗⌗ and his speech to Nut, which is repeated also on the sarcophagus and coffins. The four straps on either side of this band name the gods of the West : On the right, Hapŷ, Anubis "Within the Temple," Kebhsenuef, and ⌗, while on the left are named Mestha, Anubis Within Ut, Duamutef, and Geb.

CANOPIC JAR-BOX OF IOUIYA.

CANOPIC jar-box in wood mounted on a sledge and covered with pitch and decorated with figures and hieroglyphic legends in stucco-gilt. The box is square, with a projecting curved cornice around the top; the lid is of the usual Egyptian box shape ⬚ and is decorated down the centre with two bands of inscriptions in stucco-gilt on a black ground. These inscriptions give the speech of the 𓀀𓏤𓏤𓏤𓏤, "Favoured of his Lord Amen, Iouiya" to his mother Nut that she may spread her protecting wings over him. On the top is a gilt knob bearing the name of Iouiya.

The front of the box is ornamented with standing figures of Isis and Nephthys in stucco-gilt on a black ground, with a dado below representing a panelled wall in gold, blue, red, and green. Along the top is a horizontal band of stucco-gilt with hieroglyphs in low relief, and at the sides are vertical bands with inscriptions. The line at the top gives the speech of Geb :—

while at the sides are speeches of Isis and Nephthys :—

(1)

(2)

At the top in the centre is a gilt knob inscribed with the name of Iouiya.

At the right side of the box are standing figures of Duamutef and Mestha in stucco-gilt with the same dado as on the front. Along the top is a horizontal band of stucco-gilt with an inscription reading :—

6.

On the two sides are vertical lines giving the speeches of Amen and Ra :—

(1) [hieroglyphs]

(2) [hieroglyphs]

The left side of the box is decorated with standing figures of Hapŷ and Khebsenuef facing one another in low relief in stucco-gilt with the same dado below as on the front. Along the top is a horizontal band of hieroglyphs reading :—

[hieroglyphs]

while at the sides are the speeches of Set-amentet and Anubis :—

(1) [hieroglyphs]

(2) [hieroglyphs]

On the end of the box are standing figures of Neith and Selk in low relief in stucco-gilt, with hieroglyphic legends in bands above and on either side of them. These inscriptions read :—

(1) [hieroglyphs]

(2) [hieroglyphs]

(3) [hieroglyphs]

BOOK OF THE DEAD.

A ROLL of papyrus, measuring 19 metres 70 cm. (now cut up into thirty-four sheets), containing forty chapters of the Book of the Dead, purporting to have been copied from an ancient document,[1] for Iouiya. The beginning of the roll is badly worm-eaten, but the last thirty-two sheets are perfect. The writing is in linear hieroglyphs, finely written in black ink with rubrics in red ink; the vignettes illustrating the various chapters are beautifully executed in colour, and form splendid specimens of Egyptian illuminating art. The following is a list of the vignettes and chapters found in the document.

Sheet 1. Iouiya and Touiyou adore and present offerings to Osiris. Iouiya is represented standing with arms upraised in the attitude of adoration, and wearing a transparent vest, loin cloth and long shirt. On his head is a white wig; on his chin a short false beard. Around his neck is a broad necklace composed of different coloured beads with an *ab* or "heart" amulet as pendant. On his arms are gold armlets and on his wrists gold bracelets with coloured inlay. Behind him stands Touiyou, clad in a long white crinkled and transparent garment, wide below but fitting closely round the waist. On her head is a long black wig, and large circular gold earrings are in her ears. Around her neck is a broad necklace, and she wears armlets and bracelets. In her right hand she holds a sistrum, and in her left a large garland composed of papyrus and lotus flowers and persea fruits. Before Iouiya is a mat with offerings of joints, ducks, bread, grapes, and vegetables spread upon it; and at the side of the mat three sealed-up wine jars

---

[1] On sheet No. 34 the papyrus ends with a note running :—

with lotus flowers twined around them.　Above the offerings is a mutilated inscription in four vertical lines, explanatory of the scene :—

"(1) Giving adoration to Osiris, kissing the ground before (2) Unnefer, said "by the Divine Father (3) of the Lord of the Two lands, the favoured "of the Good God Iou (4) iya, justified."

In front of the offerings and figures is Osiris seated upon a throne and dais.　The god wears the white crown with feathers on either side and a long false beard.　Around his neck is a broad necklace composed of bands of different coloured beads.　He is clad in a long close-fitting garment, wears bracelets upon his wrists, and holds the ⌡-sceptre and scourge.　Above him are three mutilated vertical lines of hieroglyphs naming Osiris and giving his titles.

Sheets　2–5.　Chapters I and XVII, with vignette of Isis and Nebhat in a canoe drawn to the town by a yoke of oxen.

Sheets　6, 7.　Chapter　XVIII.
　,,　　　,,　　　,,　　LXXXIII, with the *bennu*-bird as vignette.
　,,　　　,,　　　,,　　LXXXIV, with the *shenti*-bird as vignette.
　,,　　　,,　　　,,　　LXXXV, with the *ba*-bird as vignette.

Sheet　8.　Chapter　LXXVII, with the gold hawk as vignette.
　,,　　　,,　　　,,　　LXXXVI, with the *ment*-bird as vignette.
　,,　　　,,　　　,,　　LXXXII, with vignette of Ptah, holding an *uas*-sceptre.

Sheet　9.　Chapter　LXXXVII, with a snake as vignette.
　,,　　　,,　　　,,　　LXXXIA, with a lotus-flower as vignette.
　,,　　　,,　　　,,　　LXIIIA, with a vignette of Iouiya kneeling and holding a cup before a tree.
　,,　　　,,　　　,,　　LXIV.

Sheets 9, 10.　Chapter　CXLI.

Sheets 10, 11. Chapter　CXC.

Sheet   11.   Chapter CIV.
   „   „   „   CIII.
   „   „   „   CXVIII.
   „   „   „   CXVII.
   „   „   „   CXIX.

Sheet   12.   Chapter CXLVIII, with vignette of a series of green-coloured
                          cows.

Sheets 12, 13. Chapter CXXXVIIA ("Chapters of the four flames," in-
                          complete).

Sheet   13.   Chapter CLV.
   „   „   „   CLVI.

Sheets 14, 15. Chapter CLIIIA, with vignette.

Sheets 16, 17. Chapter LXIV.

Sheet   18.   Chapter CX, with vignettes.

Sheet   19.   Chapter ?

Sheets 19, 20. Chapter CXLIV, with vignettes.

Sheets 20, 21. Chapter CXLV.

Sheets 21, 22. Chapter CXLVI, with vignettes.

Sheets 22, 23. Chapter XCIX, with vignettes.

Sheets 24, 25. Chapter CXXV.   Introduction.

Sheets 26–28.   Chapter CXXV.   Negative Confession.

Sheet   29.   Chapter C, with vignette.
   „   „   „   CII.

Sheets 29, 30. Chapter CXXXVIB.
   „   „   „   CXXXVI (II).

Sheets 30–33.   Chapter CXLIXA–O.

Sheets 33, 34. Chapter CL, with vignette.

THE SARCOPHAGUS OF TOUIYOU.

THE mummy of Touiyou was enclosed in two separate coffins nested one within the other, and placed in a large rectangular wooden sarcophagus mounted on a sledge.

The sledge and sarcophagus are both of a coarse-grained wood covered with pitch and decorated with figures and hieroglyphic legends in stucco-gilt. In shape the sarcophagus is rectangular, with a lid in the form of a projecting curved cornice and top of the common Egyptian box shape ⬚ Like the sarcophagus of Iouiya, the joints are mortice- and tenon-pinned.

Down the lid are three vertical columns of hieroglyphs, one in the centre and two on either side, giving prayers to Nut, reading :—

(1) In the centre :

(2) On the right side :

(3) On the left side :

At the top end of the lid, between the vertical columns of hieroglyphs, are the sacred eyes and figures of Anubis :—

At the lower end are two inscriptions, reading :—

(1) [hieroglyphs]   (2) [hieroglyphs]

At the top end of the box are two vertical and one horizontal bands of hieroglyphs, and a figure of Nephthys with arms upraised, standing upon a *nub*-sign.   The inscriptions read :—

(1) [hieroglyphs]

(2) [hieroglyphs]

(3) [hieroglyphs]

At the lower end of the box are two vertical and one horizontal bands of hieroglyphs, and a figure of Isis with arms upraised, standing upon a *nub*-sign.   The inscriptions read :—

(1) [hieroglyphs]

(2) [hieroglyphs]

(3) [hieroglyphs]

On the right side of the box are two vertical and one horizontal bands of inscriptions, and a procession of the four gods of the West.   The inscriptions read :—

(1) [hieroglyphs]

(2) [hieroglyphs]

(3) [hieroglyphs]

On the left side of the box are also two vertical and one horizontal bands of inscriptions, and a procession of the four gods of the West. The inscriptions read :—

(1) [hieroglyphs]

[hieroglyphs]

[hieroglyphs]

(2) [hieroglyphs]

(3) [hieroglyphs]

The interior of the sarcophagus is decorated with figures and inscriptions. On one end is a figure of Isis with arms upraised, and kneeling upon a *nub*-sign, while on the other end is delineated Nephthys in a similar attitude. The texts on the sides of the box give the following chapters from the Book of the Dead, with unimportant variants :—

Chapter I.

„　　XIV.

„　　XXVI.

„　　XXVII.

„　　XXXв.

„　　LXXII.

„　　XCII.

„　　CV.

OUTER COFFIN OF TOUIYOU.

THE outer coffin, consisting of lid and box, is made of wood carved and covered with stucco-gilt. It is mummiform in shape, the wig is long and the hair represented by bands of incised lines. The features of the face are very finely modelled. The eyes, eyelashes, and eyebrows are inlaid ; the eyes are of white marble and obsidian, the eyelashes and eyebrows of opaque violet glass.

Suspended from the neck is a necklace, and upon the chest is a pectoral ; from this pectoral the hands, which are closed, protrude, the right wrist being crossed on the left, while on the right wrist is a broad bracelet. The necklace and pectoral are composed of ten bands of conventional flowers and petals inlaid in coloured glasses, with hawk-headed " spreading-pieces " at the ends.

Upon the abdomen is a figure of the goddess Nut, kneeling on one knee and with winged arms outspread. Down the lower part of the abdomen and the whole length of the legs are two vertical columns of hieroglyphs, beginning : (1) [hieroglyphs] "Speech of the Royal Mother of the Great Royal Wife, the Royal Ornament, the Favourite of the Good God, the Lady Touiyou, justified," and giving the usual prayer to Nut for her protection.

Around the sides of the lid and box are represented the so-called mummy-straps, giving the same formulae as are found on the coffins of Iouiya.

Upon the wig, at the top of the head, is a figure of the goddess Nephthys with arms upraised, kneeling on a *neb*-sign. On the soles of the feet is a figure of Isis with upraised arms, kneeling upon a *nub*-sign, with a vertical line of inscription on either side of her, reading :—

(1) [hieroglyphs]   (2) [hieroglyphs] *sic*

Below are two *ded*-signs.

7.

INNER COFFIN OF TOUIYOU.

THE inner coffin consists of a lid and a box carved in wood and covered with stucco-gilt. It is mummiform in shape, the wig is long and the hair represented by bands of incised lines. Like the face of the outer coffin, the features of the face are very finely modelled, and the eyes, eyebrows and eyelashes are inlaid in the same materials.

The broad necklace is very elaborate, and consists of fifteen rows of conventional flowers and petals and drop-shaped beads, which are inlaid in coloured glass. Hanging from the neck and resting on the broad necklace is a rectangular pectoral in stucco-gilt, with a *kheper*-sign in the centre, a circle above and ring below, with a *ded*-sign on one side and a *sa*-sign on the other : this pectoral is suspended by a double chain of drop-shaped beads alternating with circular ones.

Upon the abdomen is a figure of the goddess Nut kneeling on one knee and with winged arms outspread. Down the front of the legs is a vertical line of hieroglyphics, beginning : 𓏺𓇋𓈖𓏏𓊠𓀭𓏏𓄿𓇌𓏤𓈖𓅱𓆓𓅆 " Speech of the Royal Ornament, the Lady, the Chantress of Amen, Touiyou," and giving the prayer to Nut for her protection.

Around the sides of the lid and box are represented the so-called mummy-straps, giving the same formulae as are found on the coffins of Iouiya. In vertical lines between these straps are given in incised hieroglyphs certain chapters of the Book of the Dead. On the right side of the body Chapter XXVI,[1] " Chapter whereby the Heart is given to a person in the Netherworld," and on the left side, Chapter XXX, " Chapter whereby the heart of a person is not kept back from him in the Netherworld," and the first part of Chapter CXII, " Chapter whereby one knoweth the powers of Pu."

---

[1] Incomplete at the end.

Upon the wig, at the top of the head, is the figure of the goddess Nephthys with arms upraised, and kneeling upon a *nub*-sign. On either side of her are vertical lines of hieroglyphs, reading :—

Beneath the feet is a figure of Isis with arms upraised, standing upon a *nub*-sign, with the following inscription on either side of her :—

Below are two *ded*-signs.

MASK AND MUMMY-STRAPS OF TOUIYOU.

MASK of Touiyou for fitting over the head of her mummy. This mask is made of several layers of coarse linen glued together and coated with plaster. The inside is bitumened, the exterior is gilt. The wig is long, lined, and with bands at the ends ; it is secured round the top of the head by a broad fillet composed of a band of lotus petals with a lotus flower and two buds on the forehead. The face is very beautifully modelled; the eyes, eyebrows, and eyelashes, like those in the mask of Iouiya, are inlaid, and of the same material. The pectoral is of stucco-gilt with inlay of coloured glasses : it consists of six rows of conventional flowers and petals and drop-shaped beads. Over the front of the mask appears to have been fastened (? by gum-arabic) a black veil of very fine texture, which has been broken away in places.

Fixed over the wrappings of Touiyou were mummy-straps firmly secured by string behind. They are cut out of a piece of linen which forms the framework, and this is covered with stucco and gilt.

At the top is a figure of Nut with wings outspread, and on either side of her are the amulets 𓊽 and 𓋴. The band running vertically down the chest gives the name and titles of Touiyou, with the speech to Nut, which is repeated also on the sarcophagus and coffins. On either side of this central band are four straps with inscriptions naming the gods of the West, and between them are figures of those deities as well as of Isis and Nephthys. Outside these, again, are two bands of inscriptions giving the same speeches of Nut which are found on the sarcophagus.

CANOPIC JAR-BOX OF TOUIYOU.

CANOPIC jar-box in wood, mounted on a sledge, and coated with pitch and decorated with figures and hieroglyphic legends in stucco-gilt. The box is square, with a projecting curved cornice around the top; the lid is of the usual Egyptian box shape ⌂ and is decorated with bands of inscription in stucco-gilt on a black ground.

The front of the box is decorated with standing figures of Isis and Nephthys in low relief, in stucco-gilt, with bands of inscriptions at the top and sides, and a panelled dado in stucco-gilt below. The inscriptions at the sides give the speeches of Isis and Nephthys, and at the top the name and titles of Touiyou.

(1) [hieroglyphs]

(2) [hieroglyphs]

(3) [hieroglyphs]

At the top, in the centre, is a gilt knob with the title ⌣ and name of Touiyou.

On the right side of the box are standing figures of Mestha and Hapŷ facing one another. The inscriptions at the sides give their speeches, and in the line above is the speech of Amentet :—

(1) [hieroglyphs]

(2) [hieroglyphs]

(3) [hieroglyphs]

On the left side of the box are standing figures of Duamutef and Khebsenuef in stucco-gilt, facing one another, with bands of inscriptions giving the name and title of Touiyou, above and at the sides the speeches of Duamutef and Khebsenuef:—

(1) [hieroglyphs]

(2) [hieroglyphs]

(3) [hieroglyphs]

On the end of the box are standing figures of Neith and Selk facing one another, with bands of inscriptions giving the speeches of Set-amentet, Neith, and Selk:—

(1) [hieroglyphs]

(2) [hieroglyphs]

(3) [hieroglyphs]

Enclosed in the Canopic jar-box were the four canopic jars containing the visceræ of the dead, each one being under the protection of a goddess and the four genii of the West. These vases are of an aragonite, finely carved, and each with lids in the shape of human heads. The visceræ are carefully wrapped up in linen bands, and pressed so as to take the shape of a mummy, and each one is surmounted by a small human-headed mask in canvas stucco-gilt.

The vase containing the stomach was under the protection of Mestha, and bears four vertical lines of incised hieroglyphs, reading:—

(1) [hieroglyphs]

(2) [hieroglyphs]

(3) [hieroglyphs]

(4) [hieroglyphs]

That containing the intestines was watched over by Hapŷ, and the lines upon it read :—

(1) [hieroglyphs]

(2) [hieroglyphs]

(3) [hieroglyphs]

(4) [hieroglyphs]

The lungs were under the protection of Tiuamautef, and the jar containing them bears the following inscriptions :—

(1) [hieroglyphs] (2) [hieroglyphs] (3) [hieroglyphs]

[hieroglyphs] (4) [hieroglyphs]

The vase containing the liver was guarded by Kebhsenuef, and the inscription upon it reads :—

(1) [hieroglyphs] (2) [hieroglyphs] (3) [hieroglyphs]

[hieroglyphs] (4) [hieroglyphs]

FUNERARY STATUETTES OF IOUIYA AND TOUIYOU.

EIGHTEEN funerary statuettes in the form of a mummy (fourteen bearing the name of Iouiya and four the namè of Touiyou) were found : they are all of exceptionally fine modelling and carving. Of those bearing the name of Touiyou, two are of wood plated with gold, and two of wood plated with silver, having gold-plated faces, hands and pectorals. Of those in-scribed with the name of Iouiya, two are of ebony, one is of pine, eight are of cedar, and two are of a commoner wood painted to imitate cedar. The specimen figured is of carved wood, with the face and body covered with two plates of beaten copper pinned down on either side. The wig is cut in the wood, is short, and painted black. The features are exquisitely modelled, and the eyes are painted with white pupils and black irises. The pectoral is formed of a band of stucco-gilt, and from the neck is suspended an *ab* or heart amulet. In the right hand is a ⸸-baton, and in the left the ⸸-thong. None of the figures are represented, as is usual with funerary statuettes, with the pick, hoe, and basket ; but a set of models of these implements was found alongside the figures. These models comprise three pairs of copper baskets, twelve yokes of wood, twelve hoes, twelve picks, and a brick-mould. This latter is of considerable interest, and was very rarely laid with the other implements.[1]

The inscription engraved upon these funerary statuettes is the usual *Shawabti* text, which forms the Sixth Chapter of the Book of the Dead, with some unimportant variants in the spelling of words. The text gives instructions whereby the statuette may be made to do the work for a person

[1] A text on a funerary statuette of the Seventeenth Dynasty found at Drah abu'l Negga runs : "If thou art called to do any work in the Underworld of a person according to his duties (either) to carry water, *to make bricks*, to carry sand from west to east, &c."

in the Netherworld.   The name of Iouiya is spelt variously on the different figures : [hieroglyphs] , [hieroglyphs] , [hieroglyphs] , or [hieroglyphs] , and the titles given are (1) [hieroglyphs] , [hieroglyphs] , or more fully [hieroglyphs] "Divine Father" and "Divine Father of the Lord of the Two Lands," and [hieroglyphs] "Favourite of the King," and [hieroglyphs] "Favourite of the Good God."   The name of Touiyou is spelt on her four figures [hieroglyphs] , and the titles given are [hieroglyphs] , "Favoured of the Good God (*i.e.*, the King)," [hieroglyphs] "Royal Ornament," and [hieroglyphs] , "Great one of the Harâm of Amen."

Besides the eighteen funerary statuettes, thirteen wooden boxes for the figures were discovered.   These boxes are rectangular, upright-oblong in shape, with curved lid, and are painted on the outside with upright panels of red, blue, and green, divided by narrow white lines ; on the insides they are coloured with yellow paint.   Four only of the boxes are inscribed.   One of them bears a vertical inscription down the front giving the *De hetep seten*, "May-the-King-give-an-offering" formula "to Osiris, Within the West, that he may present all that which issues upon his altar for the *ka* of the Favoured of the Good God, Iouiya, justified;" on its lid is the inscription [hieroglyphs] "Devoted towards Osiris Yau, justified."   The three other inscribed boxes bear a similar text upon the lid but the names and title of Iouiya are written [hieroglyphs] "The Divine Father, Áaaï."

ALABASTER VASE BEARING THE NAMES OF AMENOPHIS III AND QUEEN THYI.

LARGE vase in alabaster, with foot, spherical body, neck, and cover. The neck is long, curves outwards towards the top, and terminates in a narrow projecting rim. The cover or cap is hemispherical in shape, with a slightly projecting rim curving outwards and fitting the rim of the neck of the vase. The belly of the vase is spherical, and rests on a narrow circular foot.

On the neck is inscribed in incised hieroglyphs the prenomen and nomen of Amenôphis III with his titles and the name and titles of Queen Thŷï. The alabaster or aragonite from which the vase is carved is of exceptionally fine quality.

MAGICAL FIGURE OF IOUIYA.

WITH the funerary statuettes was found a single figure, mummiform in shape and beautifully carved in cedar-wood, bearing down its front two vertical columns of incised hieroglyphs, the first giving, in an abbreviated form, the text of the "Chapter of the Flame" from the Book of the Dead (Ch. CLI f.) ; the second, a shortened version of the "Chapter of the Magical Figure of the Northern Wall," from the Book of the Dead (Ch. CLI, d.). The bases of similar figures were found by Mr. Davis in the Tomb of Thoutmôsis IV (Carter and Newberry, *The Tomb of Thoutmôsis IV*, p. 9).

ALABASTER VASE.

LARGE vase in alabaster, with foot, spherical body, neck, and handle. The neck is long and terminated by a wide projecting rim ; the handle is connected at the neck and bends downwards towards the belly ; the foot is circular.

The alabaster is stained as with some oily substance that was no doubt contained in it. The mouth was covered with a piece of linen, which was tied by a strand of string secured by a pellet of clay and sealed.

ALABASTER VASE.

V<small>ASE</small> in alabaster, with foot, spherical body, neck, and handle. The neck is long, cylindrical in shape, and terminates in a wide projecting rim. The handle is connected at the top of the neck below the rim, and bends downwards towards the belly, where it terminates in two papyrus flowers, delicately cut. The belly is spherical, resembling a mace-head in shape, and rests on a narrow projecting foot, a third of which has been chipped away.

The alabaster is of fine quality and very delicately carved. On the upper part of the handle are the remains of a piece of linen used for securing the vase's contents.

DUMMY VASES.

Besides the vases in alabaster, there were found in the tomb of Iouiya and Touiyou twenty-seven "dummy" vases in wood and terra-cotta, painted to represent alabaster, glass, black and white diorite, and red breccia.

The shapes of these dummy vases are various, ranging from the plain cylindrical vase with projecting rim, to the long-necked vase with spherical body and long handle. The number of the various forms may be grouped as follows :—

Four coloured to imitate alabaster; two representing blue glass with yellow wave lines, and two dark blue glass with band of lotus petals around the neck.

Two coloured to represent blue-green glass with yellow wave lines; two representing blue glass with yellow wave lines and rosettes; six representing alabaster, and one of pottery painted white and varnished, the varnish having turned a bright brown. Of this form there are also two wooden vases, painted to imitate alabaster with a band of lotus petals around the upper part of the belly.

Of this type of vase there are eight specimens, all of them painted to represent black and white diorite, or red and white breccia. Around the neck of one of the vases of this form is painted a band of lotus petals.

AMULETS.

AMBER SCARAB inscribed with a magical text in five horizontal lines of hieroglyphs, and bearing the name of Touiyou. On the base at the top is incised the hieroglyphic [glyph], and the text reads :—

(1) [hieroglyphs] (2) [hieroglyphs] (3) [hieroglyphs]

(4) [hieroglyphs] (5) [hieroglyphs]

SCARAB-AMULET in dark blue glass to imitate lapis lazuli and exquisitely modelled. It stands upon a green beryl base, to which it is cemented by a thick layer of cement. The base is inscribed with the text of the Chapter of the Heart from the Book of the Dead, in ten horizontal lines of hieroglyphs. The first line gives the name of Touiyou [hieroglyphs] "Touiyou she says," and the second begins [hieroglyphs] "*He* says My heart." The duplication of the word [glyph] and the alteration of the third person suffix from feminine to masculine, shows that this scarab was originally made for a man, and that the name of Touiyou was inserted afterwards.

SCARAB-AMULET in green beryl, with head chipped, and inscribed with the Chapter of the Heart from the Book of the Dead. It bears the name of Touiyou.

Ded-AMULET of wood, stuccoed and gilt, and inscribed with the name and titles of Touiyou, and the text of the 155th Chapter of the Book of the Dead :—

(1) [hieroglyphs] (2) [hieroglyphs] (3) [hieroglyphs]

[hieroglyphs] (4) [hieroglyphs]

Ded-AMULET in blue faïence, with narrow bands of gold-foil at the top, centre, and bottom.

Sa-AMULET of red jasper, inscribed with a magical text reading :—

(1) [hieroglyphs] (2) [hieroglyphs]

(3) [hieroglyphs]

Ba-BIRD in wood, painted and inscribed upon the base with the name of Touiyou.

SEALINGS in clay, with impressions of an oval-shaped seal representing a recumbent Anubis, with nine prisoners with arms tied behind them below.

MODEL MIRROR, with plain handle of wood, stucco-gilt, and plate made of canvas, stuccoed and coloured blue.

KOHL-TUBE in light blue-glazed faïence, with a vertical line of hieroglyphs in dark violet glaze inlay, giving the names and titles of Amenôphis III: [hieroglyphs]. This Kohl-tube is fitted with an ebony needle, and stoppered with a piece of papyrus pith ; it is slightly chipped at the mouth of the tube.

THE CHARIOT.

THE chariot bears no name, but we may presume that it belonged to Iouiya. It is in nearly perfect preservation : the framework of the body, the wheels and the pole, are intact, and even the leather-work which has been stripped from the sides of the "body" has been found, and could be put back in place. It is doubtful whether it was ever used except for the funeral procession, for the leather tyres are hardly scratched.

The body, 90 cm. in breadth, consists of a semicircular framework half open at the back, with a floor of leather mesh-work for the charioteer to stand on. The floor is formed of a bent rod with rectangular holes, through which the leather mesh-work is lashed, while the back piece consists of a board about an inch in thickness, to the front of which, through holes, the leather mesh-work is lashed, and underneath which the butt end of the pole is fastened. The front of the body consists of a bent rod or rail above, supported by ten wooden uprights arranged at equal distances. The body is supported by the pole and by the axletree : its front is lashed to the pole which is carried under the centre of the body to the back-piece of the floor in which the butt end of the pole is fastened. The back is supported by the axletree, to which it is bound at the ends and at four equal intervals between. The axletree is made out of a solid beam about two-and-a-half inches thick.

The wheels are 75 cm. in diameter and are six-spoked ; the spokes are morticed and tenoned into a nave, 7 cm. in diameter, formed by a hollow wooden cylinder, through which the axletree runs. The wheels are kept in place by lynch pins outside and by the thickness of the axletree on the inside. The rim of the wheel is formed of two pieces of bent wood lashed together, the lashings being covered by stucco-gilt. The tyre of the wheel is made of strips of leather sewn together and stained red, with leather padding below.

The pole is about 2 metres long, and 6 cm. from the end is a hole, to which the yoke was pinned by a wooden peg and lashed.   The yoke is made of a single piece of bent wood, with round knobs at the ends and four bands of stucco-gilt at equal intervals around it.   The pole is bent into an elbow, where it meets the body and then flattens out to a breadth of 5 cm.   It is dovetailed into the back-piece of the body, whilst in front it is lashed to the frame of the body, the lashings being covered with stucco-gilt.

The front, sides, and back of the body were filled in, above, by two sheets of red leather with green and white appliqué border, fixed by copper pins, and below, by leather stuccoed and gilt with decoration in low relief in imitation of embossed leather-work.   This decoration consisted, in the centre, of two goats browsing upon a conventional " tree of life," with a row of rosettes running along the sides and bands of coil patterns on either side, and panels at the ends with "trees of life" made out of conventionalised lotus flowers.   At the back, on the left-hand side, the upper part is filled in with plain red leather with appliqué border, and below is a panel of rosettes framed by a coil-pattern border with a conventional "tree of life" on the left-hand side.

GILT STUCCO PANELS FROM BED.

DETAIL OF CARVED CHAIR BACK.

CHAIR OF PRINCESS SAT-AMEN.

THE largest and most elaborate of the three chairs bears the name of Sat-amen, daughter of Amenôphis III by Queen Tîyi, and consequently a granddaughter of Iouiya and Touiyou.

The chair is made of wood, the various parts being fixed together by mortice and tenon joints, pegged. It is 77 cm. high ; the seat is 34 cm. from the ground, 52 cm. wide, and 54 cm. deep. The back and frame of the seat are constructed of a common wood veneered with a rarer one, probably walnut ; the veneer is about one-eighth of an inch thick, and is pinned down with small wooden pins. The legs are carved out of solid blocks of walnut. The back is high, curved to fit the body, slopes outwards towards the top and is supported at the back by three uprights rising vertically from the back of the frame of the seat. The arms are built of a frame of solid wood containing a panel, the upper pieces of the frame curving upwards to the back of the chair. Upon the top of the frame is a moulding of wood gilt, projecting slightly over the thickness of the arm ; it is pegged to it and carried in a curve to the top of the back, and ends in front in finely carved gilded busts, which are pegged on to the frame of the seat. The seat is composed of plaited string threaded through holes in the framework and tied beneath. It is supported on four legs, carved to represent the fore and hind legs of a lion, the feet of which rest on small ▽-shaped bases covered with silver-foil. Between the two front legs and the two back legs are cross-bars rounded, and terminating with bands of gold at the ends, while attached to the frame immediately beneath the seat is a curved support to give extra strength to the seat.

The decoration (see fig. 1) is modelled in gesso and gilt.   On the back it consists of a winged disc with uraei and the name ⛨ "Edfu" on either side.   Below this is a rectangular panel containing a scene in duplicate ←⚔→, showing Sat-amen seated receiving an offering of a gold necklace from a female slave or attendant.   The inscription above the Princess reads : "The eldest daughter of the king whom he loves, Sat-amen," while that above the slave explains the scene "offering gold of the lands of the South." The whole is framed at the top and on either side by a band of rectangles with a frieze of hanging lotus flowers and buds.

FIG. 1. DECORATION ON BACK OF THE CHAIR OF PRINCESS SAT-AMEN.

The Princess is clad in a close-fitting vest and a long crimped skirt reaching to the ankles.   She wears a short wig, secured round the top of the head by a narrow fillet tied behind in a bow : over the forehead is a small gazelle head with horns.   Upon the top of the head is a crown, consisting of a disc, from which issue three lotus flowers with buds between.   From this crown hang flaps, one on either side of the head, reaching to the breasts. In her ears are earrings, and around her neck is a broad necklace, consisting of three bands of lotus petals.   On the wrists are bracelets, and in her right hand she holds a sistrum and in her left a *menat*.   The chair that she is seated on has a high back, and its arms are shown covered with a scale pattern ; its legs are modelled after the fashion of those of the lion.   The chair is placed on a large mat, and a small one is represented beneath the Princess's feet.

The slave or attendant is clad in a close-fitting vest and long skirt ornamented by horizontal decorated bands.   She wears a short wig, secured by a fillet over the forehead with bow tied behind, and on the top of it is a disc.   In her ears are earrings ; around her neck is a broad necklace and on her wrists are bracelets.   She holds before her in her two hands a mat with broad gold necklace or pectoral upon it.

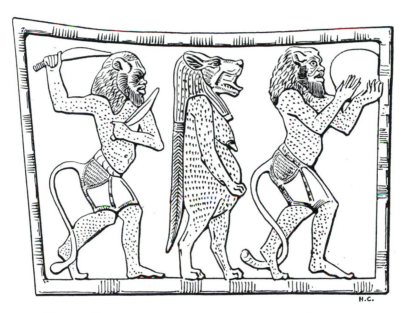

FIG. 2.   LEFT-HAND PANEL OF ARM OF CHAIR OF SAT-AMEN.

The scene is continued in the panels on the insides of the arms, where four female slaves are depicted bearing offerings of gold rings.   These females are clad in elaborately ornamented embroidered or tapestry-woven garments, and wear discs on their heads consisting of three lotus flowers or of three rosettes.

On the outside panels of the arms are also scenes in gesso gilt.   On the one (fig. 2) is a figure of Tauris standing between two dancing figures of Bes.   The first figure shows the god of music clad in a short skirt dancing to the strains of a tambourine, which he is beating with his right hand. The second figure depicts him armed with two knives and dancing a jig. On the other are three figures of Bes dancing (see fig. 3).

These scenes of Bes and Thueris (the latter, it should be remarked, is *lion*,[1] not hippopotamus-headed) are interesting. Bes dancing to the notes of his tambourine is a motive already known to us from some small faïence figures and ring bezels found in the ruins of the Palace of Amenôphis III at Thebes, and in the town of Akhenaten at Tell el Amarna. The attitude and liveliness of these figures is unlike anything else that we know of Upper Egyptian art, and suggests a Delta or perhaps a foreign origin. But, unfortunately, we know as yet too little about the civilisation of the Eastern Mediterranean at this date (B.C. 1400) to allow of anything definite being said on the subject. Already in the time of Thoutmôsis III several new motives are found in Egyptian art, due no doubt to the trade relations that

FIG. 3.   RIGHT-HAND PANEL OF ARM OF CHAIR OF SAT-AMEN.

had sprung up between the peoples of Western Asia and Egypt. At a slightly later period foreign artisans were brought to the Nile Valley and introduced the arts of glass-making and tapestry-weaving, and the

[1] The lion-headed Thueris is otherwise unknown in Egyptian art. Professor Bosanquet has kindly supplied me with the following notes on the subject :—

"The appearance of a lion-headed goddess on a piece of furniture made in Egypt in the reign of Amenôphis III supplies a fresh confirmation of the view that the lion-headed demons of Mycenæan art were ultimately derived from Egypt. Dr. Winter connected them with the Egyptian hippopotamus-goddess, Thueris.[1] Dr. Arthur Evans has proposed a different name, that of Ririt, the female hippopotamus, which in Egyptian art stands for the constellation known to us as 'Charles' Wain.'[2] The design on the chair of Princess Sat-amen shows the transition from the hippopotamus-head to the lion-head, already

[1] *Jahrbuch des k. d. Archäol. Instituts*, V (1890), p. 108 (Anzeiger).
[2] *Journal of Hellenic Studies*, XXI (1891), p. 169.

extraordinary proficiency which they displayed shows that their skill must have been the result of generations of work and experience. To what civilisation these foreign workmen belonged we do not as yet know for certain, and it is perhaps fruitless to conjecture until explorations have been made on sites in the Delta and in other countries bordering on the Mediterranean.

accomplished on Egyptian soil. The Mycenæan figures which Winter explained as blundering imitations of the Thueris type are as follows :—

(A) A pair of demons holding ewers, repeated three times on each handle of a bronze vessel found in Cyprus and preserved in the New York Museum.[3] Of all the Mycenæan examples these come nearest to the Egyptian figure on the chair ; they wear on shoulders and back a continuation of the lion's mane, forming a back-covering somewhat broader and longer than that of the Egyptian figure, but otherwise, as Mr. Myres was the first to remark, exceedingly like it. There is no sign of feminine breasts.

(B) Three figures with apparently asinine heads, bearing on their shoulders a pole, painted on a fragment of wall-plaster found at Mycenæ.[4] Their tongues loll out, and give the same effect in profile as the tuft of hair under the chins of the lion-headed demons on the bronze vase. They wear the same shaggy back-covering, but in this case it is confined about the waist by a belt, and was certainly understood by the painter as a detachable garment.

(C) A series of glass plaques found by Tsountas at Mycenæ, representing pairs of lion-headed figures holding ewers. Between them rises in most cases a cairn or a pillar, over which they seem about to pour a libation.[5] The back-covering is always belted.

(D) Zöocephalous demons, single or in pairs, on engraved gems. On a gem found at Vaphio they stand face to face holding ewers, about to water a palm-tree growing in a pot at their feet ; in two cases a single ewer-bearer is represented.[6] On a lentoid gem from Mycenæ a similar demon, without the ewer, stands between two supporting lions,[7] On another lentoid the ewer-bearing demons act as supporters at either side of a human figure.[8] Other stones show the demon carrying slaughtered animals on a pole, or lifting on his shoulders a dead bull.[9] In most cases the belt as well as the hairy back-covering is distinctly represented. The latest addition to the series is a much-worn cylinder from Palaikastro in Crete, on which the lion-headed demon is associated with two female figures and two trees.[10]

The adoption of this Egyptian type and its diffusion through the Minoan world was no doubt due to the fact that it gave concrete expression to a belief in composite monsters which was already current there.

---

[3] Perrot and Chipiez, *Art in Phœnicia and Cyprus*, II, pp. 363, 364. *Journal of Hellenic Studies*, XIV (1894), p. 104.

[4] *Ephemeris Archaologike* (1887), Pl. X. Compare *Journal of Hellenic Studies*, XIV, pp. 81 and 101, where Mr. A. B. Cook argues that the object which they carry is a rope, not a pole, because it is covered with diagonal markings ; but comparison with other Mycenæan paintings does not confirm this view. The diagonal lines were added to distinguish the pole from the background.

[5] Published by Dr. A. J. Evans, *Journal of Hellenic Studies*, XXI, p. 117.

[6] *Journal of Hellenic Studies*, XIV (1894), p. 84, fig. 4 ; and p. 106, figs. 6, 7, 8.

[7] *Journal of Hellenic Studies*, XXI (1901), p. 168.

[8] *Journal of Hellenic Studies*, XIV, p. 120, fig. 14.

[9] *Journal of Hellenic Studies*, XIV, p. 84, figs. 2 and 3.

[10] *Annual of British School at Athens*, VIII (1902), p. 302.

CHAIR BEARING THE NAMES OF QUEEN TIYI AND PRINCESS SAT-AMEN.

THIS chair bears a scene upon the back showing Queen Tîyi and two princesses—one of whom is Sat-amen—in a papyrus canoe. Its dimensions prove that it must have been made for a child, and as the gold has been rubbed off and patched again in places, it is probable that it was used by the Princess Sat-amen when a child. The seat was originally of plaited string, which had no doubt been worn through and then cut out and a rectangular board, painted yellow, inserted.

The chair is made of a coarse-grained wood, the various parts being fixed together by mortice and tenon joints, pegged. With the exception of the seat, which is painted yellow, the whole chair is covered with stucco and gilt. The back is high, curved to fit the body, slopes outwards towards the top, and is supported at the back by the uprights rising vertically from the back of the frame of the seat. The arms are built of a frame of solid wood, the upper pieces of which curve upwards to the back of the chair. Upon the top of the frame is a moulding of wood gilt, projecting slightly over the thickness of the arm and carried down to the outside corner of the frame of the seat. Within the frame of the arms are figures of Thueris and Bes carved in the round and fixed by mortice and tenon joints above and below.

The rear is composed of a woodwork frame containing a rectangular board, painted yellow. The frame has been pierced at short intervals by small holes through which, no doubt, string was threaded to form a plaited string seat. It is supported on four legs, carved to represent the fore and hind legs of a lion, the feet of which rest on small ▽-shaped bases. Between the front pair of legs and the back pair, and attached to the frame immediately beneath the seat, is a curved support to give extra strength to the seat. The height of the back is 61 cm., of the seat 235 mm., and the depth of the seat is 35 cm.

The decoration of the chair is modelled in stucco-gilt. On the outer face of the back (see fig. 4) it consists of a scene representing Queen Tîyi and two princesses on a papyrus boat in a marsh, the whole being framed by a row of *khekar* ornaments above and a delicate coil pattern on either side. The queen is shown seated in a high-backed chair with arms. She

FIG. 4. DECORATION ON BACK OF THE CHAIR BEARING NAMES OF QUEEN TIYI AND SAT-AMEN.

is clad in a close fitting vest with long, thin and transparent crimped skirt. On her head she wears a double feathered crown and long wig. Around her neck is a broad necklace, while on her arms are armlets. In her right hand she holds an *ankh* and in her left a flail or fly-flip. Beneath her seat is seated a cat with tail erect. Above her is her name, "The Great Royal Wife Tîyi." In front of the Queen and in the prow of the canoe stands the young princess Sat-amen offering her mother a bunch of lotus flowers which

10.

she holds before her in her right hand. She is clad only in a short skirt with long girdle tie. She wears her hair short behind with long curls hanging down either side of the face. On her head is a diadem or tiara, consisting of five upright lotus flowers with long stalks, with a lotus bud hanging down over the forehead. Around her neck is a bead necklace and on her arms are armlets. In her left hand is a feather fan with long handle. Behind the Queen stands, in the stern of the canoe, a second princess, who holds before her a large fan with a garland of lotus and poppy flowers arranged up its handle. The canoe is made of papyrus stalks with papyrus and lotus flowers at prow and stern. Below it is a double row of papyrus reeds.

On the back of the chair, on a rectangular panel, is a figure of Bes with wings spread out from his sides and knives fixed to his feet. On either side of him he holds a *neb*-basket in which are *ankh* and *sa*-amulets. This figure is partly hidden by the centre wooden upright supporting the back of the chair.

OSIRIS BEDS.

In one section of the chamber of the tomb were found two " beds of Osiris," one each for the persons buried. The beds consist of a rectangular frame of wood divided by two longitudinal and six transverse bars pinned together with wooden pegs. Upon the top of the frame has been fixed a papyrus-reed mat, and over the whole a double sheet of linen has been stretched and sewn together at the ends and below in order to keep it taut. Upon the top of this, in the middle, an outline of the figure of Osiris facing to the left has been traced in ink. The surface thus outlined was sprinkled with earth and sand and afterwards sown with grains of barley. This small plantation was carefully watered till the grains germinated and grew, and then, when the young corn had reached the height of about eight inches, it was pressed flat by the whole bed being wrapped in a sheet of linen and allowed to dry before it was deposited in the tomb.

The only other example of an Osiride figure made of growing corn was that found by M. Loret in the tomb of Maa-her-pra, and has been described by M. Daressy in his Catalogue[1] of the objects found in that tomb. The signification of these " beds " is, according to Professor Wiedemann,[2] the material expression of the idea of life springing from death, as the new corn springs from the old seed laid in the ground. Osiris had vegetated in this way before his resurrection, as is seen by the pictures on the walls of the temples of the Græco-Roman period.

[1] *Catalogue Général des Antiquités Égyptiennes du Musée du Caire*, No. 24,661.

[2] Wiedemann, in an article on " Osiris végétant " in the *Museon*, nouvelle série IV, 1903 pp. 111–123. Margaret Murray, *The Osireion*, pp. 28–29.

COFFER BEARING THE NAMES OF AMENOPHIS III.

COFFER raised on four legs, consisting of a cavetto cornice and a frieze of blue glazed faïence tiles, enriched with hieroglyphic signs ♀☋↾, symbolising "Life, Stability and Power," formed in gilt gesso in low relief. The top is in two folding leaves, hinged at either side and opening in the centre, and decorated with a painted design of two ⧈-figures kneeling upon a ⌒-sign and bearing upon their heads the cartouches of Amenôphis III.

The angle-posts of the coffer are carried down to form the legs, which spread slightly towards the feet. Immediately below the frieze the whole construction is strengthened by a system of cross-bracing, in the form of king and queen post trusses. This form of construction combines the maximum of strength with the minimum amount of material.

Upon the lids are fixed wooden knobs, inscribed with the names of Amenôphis III, and on either side of these knobs are wooden ⟶-bolts running in copper-wire hoops.

Height, 51 cm.   Length, 53 cm.   Breadth, 42 cm.

COFFER BEARING THE NAMES OF AMENOPHIS III AND QUEEN THYI.

COFFER raised on four legs, consisting of a cavetto cornice and a frieze of blue glazed tiles, enriched with hieroglyphic inscriptions formed in gilt gesso in low relief. A curved segmental lid rests on the top of the cornice. The angle-posts of the coffer are continued downwards and form parallel legs with a cross rail below the frieze.

Around the ends and sides of the lid is a border of rectangles, encrusted with pieces of ebony, ivory, stained red ivory and blue glazed faïence. Within this border are two panels of blue glazed faïence divided across the middle and decorated with designs in gilt gesso, in the lower half with ⟨figure⟩-figures kneeling upon a ⟨sign⟩-sign, and in the upper half with the cartouches of Amenôphis III, surmounted by double feathers and the sun's disc with uraei.

The cavetto cornice is in stucco-gilt, and the frieze consists of a panel of blue glazed faïence tiles, with, on either side of the coffer, the titles and names of Amenôphis III, and on the ends the titles and names of Queen Thŷï, the whole being bordered above and below by a band of encrusted coloured rectangles, similar to those on the lid.

The space between the frieze and the cross rail below it is filled in with pierced ornament, consisting of a series of ⟨symbol⟩ carved in wood and gilt, and backed by stained red linen of very fine texture. The angle-posts and rails are encrusted on the outer faces with bands of coloured rectangles.

On the lid and on one end of the coffer are wooden knobs, around which the string to secure the lid was fastened.

STAFF AND WHIP.

WOODEN STAFF covered with stucco and painted black to represent ebony, and ornamented at the upper end with seven double bands of gold, representing string binding ; between the gold bands the staff is coloured alternately red and black, and in each division are five flowers with gold centres and yellow dots around to represent petals.   On the top end of the stick is incised a rosette in gold.   Down the staff is an inscription in yellow hieroglyphs, reading: [hieroglyphs] "The veteran in the service of Osiris, the favoured one of the Good God Iouiya, justified." The staff is broken at the lower end and measures 115 cm.

WHIP-HANDLE of wood with leather thong.   The handle is painted black to imitate ebony, and at the upper end is ornamented with four lines of white to imitate ivory.   Down the handle is an inscription, reading : [hieroglyphs] " The veteran in the service of Osiris, Iouiya."   The handle measures 396 cm. in length.

PLATE VI.

SARCOPHAGUS OF IOUIYA.

PLATE VII.

PLATE VIII.

SECOND COFFIN OF IOUIYA.

PLATE IX

INNER COFFIN OF IOUIYA.

PLATE X

CANOPIC-JAR BOX OF IOUIYA.

PLATE X

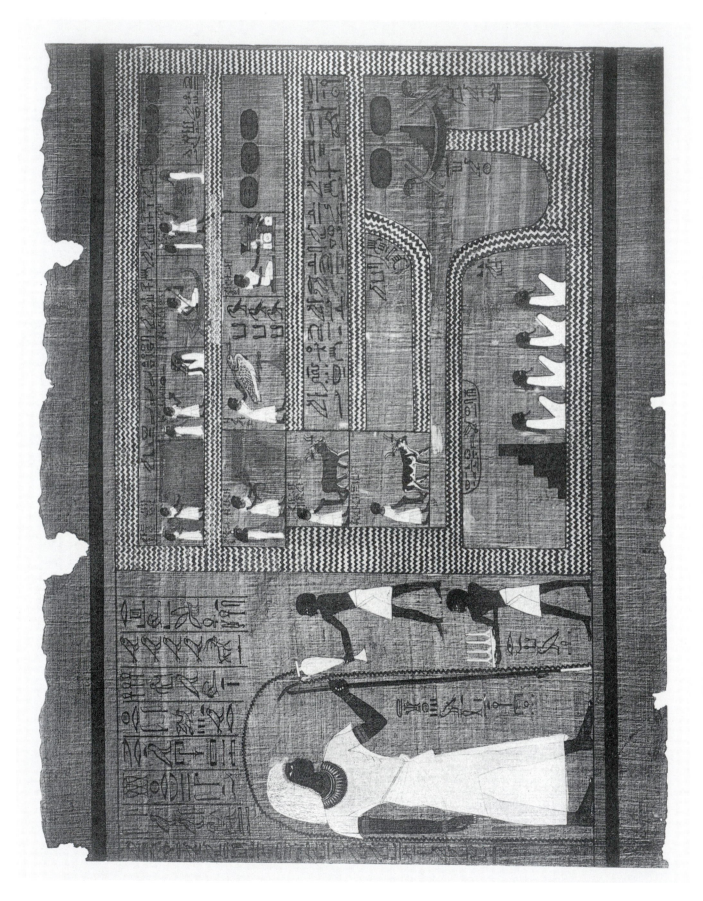

PLATE XII.

SARCOPHAGUS OF TOUIYOU.

PLATE XII

OUTER COFFIN OF TOUIYOU.

PLATE XIV.

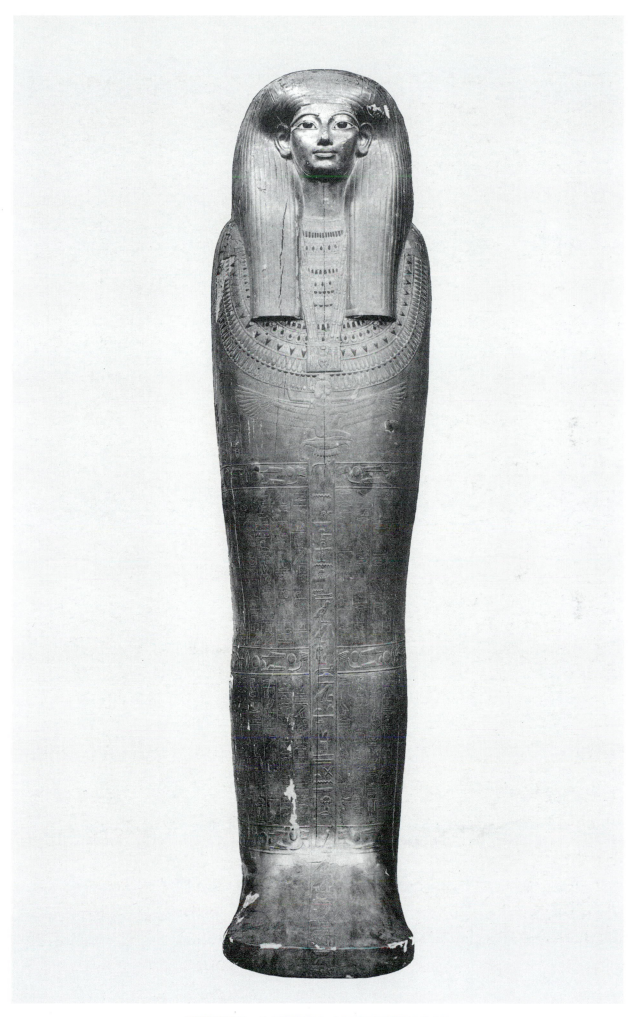

INNER COFFIN OF TOUIYOU.

PLATE XV

CARTONNAGE MASK OF TOUIYOU.

PLATE XVI.

CANOPIC-JAR BOX OF TOUIYOU.

PLATE XV

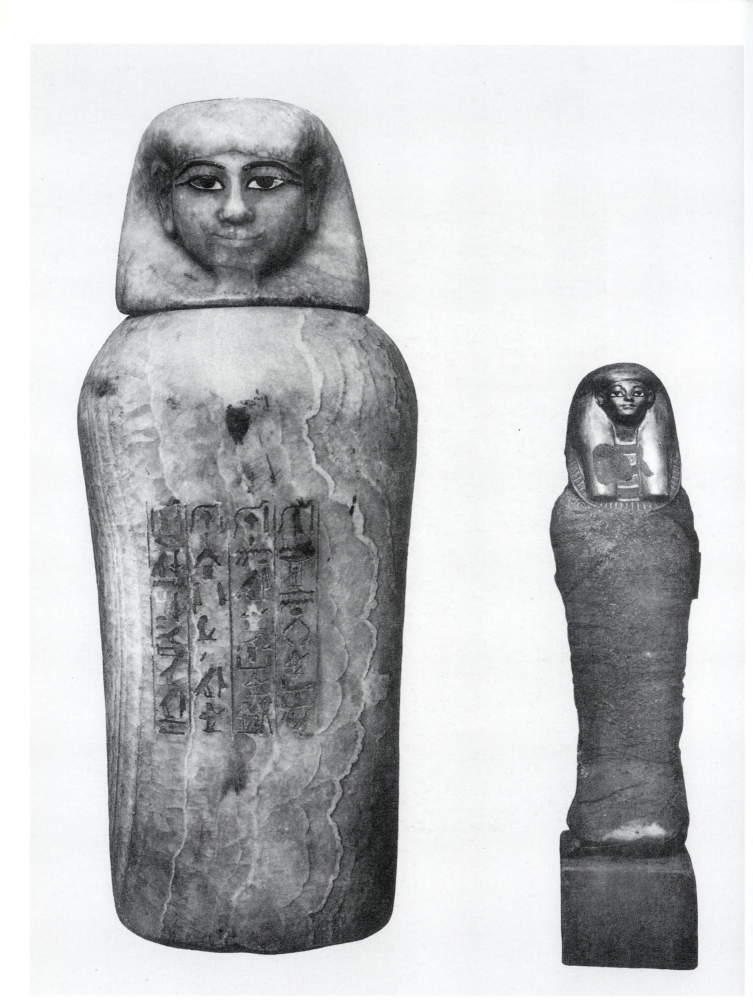

CANOPIC JAR WITH MUMMIFIED LIVER.
SURMOUNTED BY CARTONNAGE MASK

PLATE XVIII

GOLD- AND SILVER-PLATED SHAWABTI FIGURES OF TOUIYOU.

PLATE XII

WOODEN SHAWABTI FIGURE OF IOUIYA.

PLATE XX.

WOODEN SHAWABTI FIGURE OF IOUIYA WITH BOX.

PLATE XX

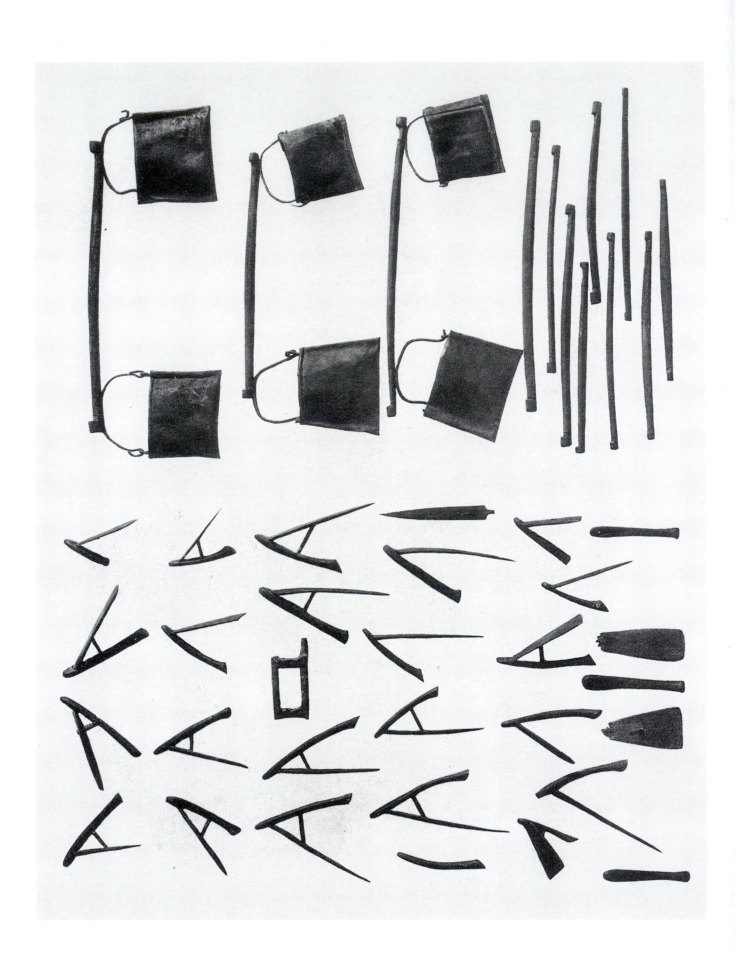

PLATE XXII

MAGICAL FIGURE OF IOUIYA.

PLATE XXI

MODEL COFFIN.
LENGTH 30 CM.

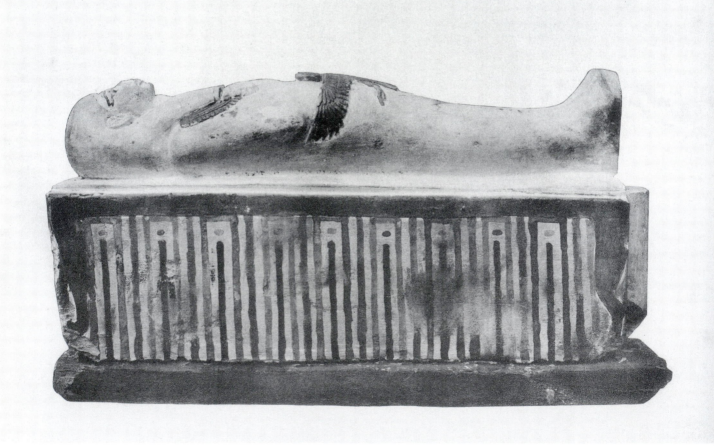

RECUMBENT FIGURE.

LENGTH 30 CM.

PLATE XXIV.

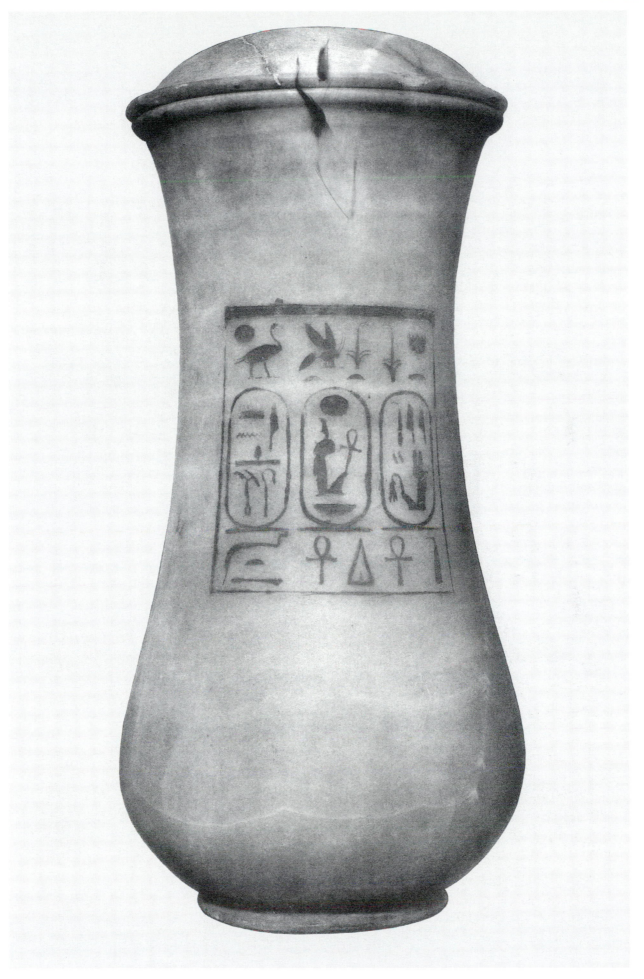

ALABASTER VASE OF AMENOPHIS III AND
QUEEN TIYI.

HEIGHT 39 CMS.

PLATE XXV

ALABASTER VASE.

HEIGHT   345 M M.

PLATE XXVI.

ALABASTER VASE.

HEIGHT 20 CM.

PLATE XXVII.

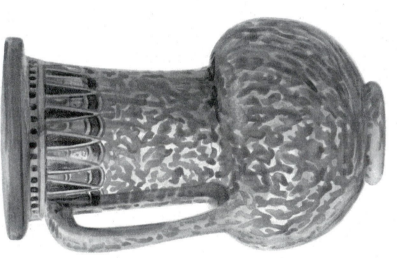

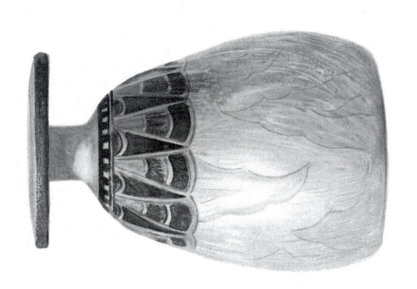

PAINTED DUMMY VASES OF WOOD.

PLATE XXVIII.

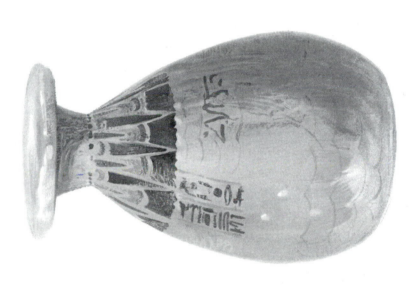

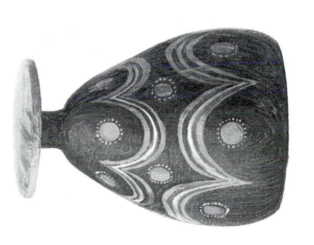

PAINTED DUMMY VASES OF WOOD.

PLATE XXIX

COFFER BEARING THE NAMES OF AMENOTHES III. AND QUEEN TIYI.

PLATE XXX

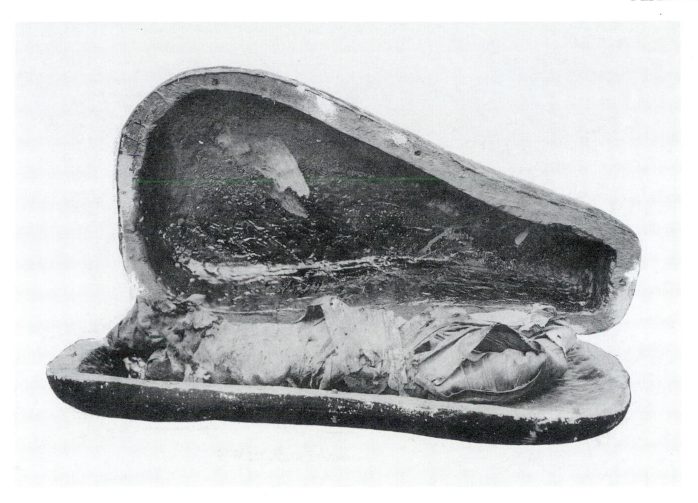

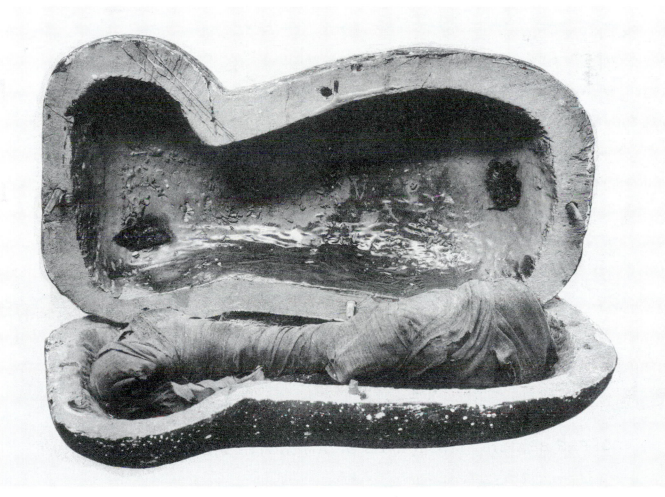

MUMMIFIED JOINTS IN WOODEN CASES.

PLATE XXXI

MUMMIFIED BIRDS IN WOODEN CASES.

PLATE XXXII

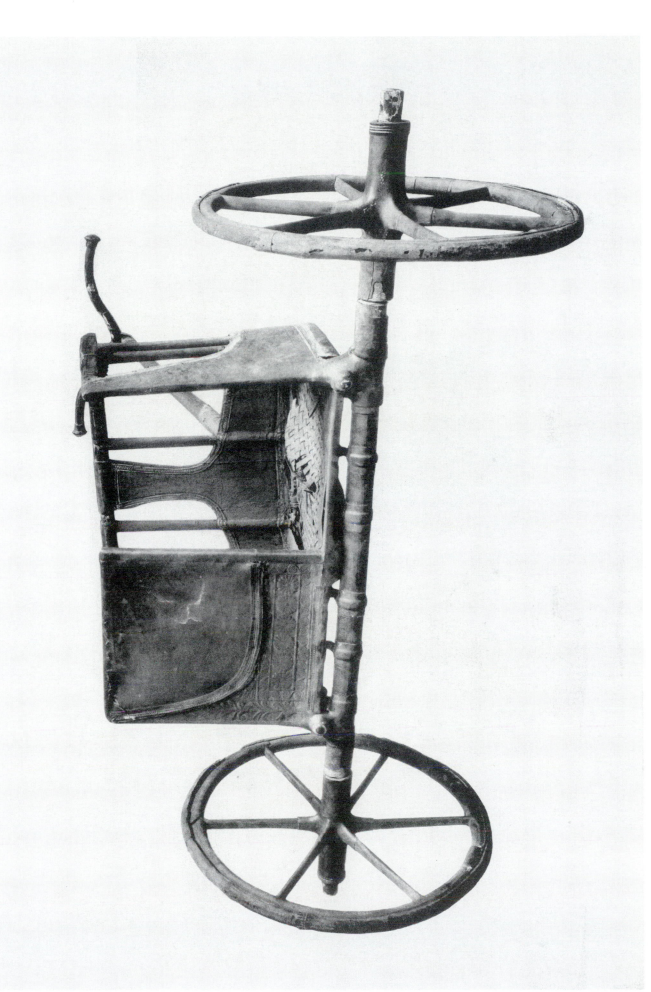

PLATE XXXIII.

CHAIR OF SAT-AMEN.

PLATE XXXIV.

BACK VIEW OF CHAIR OF SAT-AMEN.

PLATE XXXV

CHAIR WITH CUSHION.

PLATE XXXVI.

CHAIR OF TIYI & SAT-AMEN.

PLATE XXXVII.

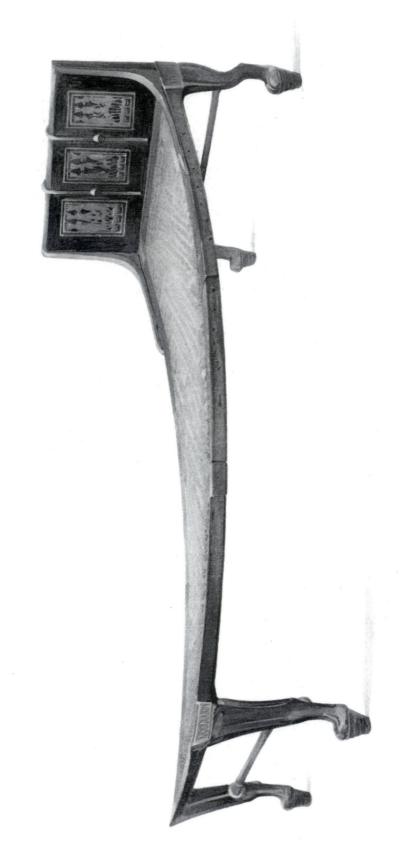

BED WITH PANELLED HEAD-PIECE.

PLATE XXXVIII.

COFFER BEARING THE NAMES OF AMENOTHES III.

PLATE XXXIX

COFFER BEARING THE NAMES OF AMENOTHES III. AND QUEEN TIYI.

PLATE XL

PAINTED WOODEN BOX OF AMENOTHES III.

LENGTH 38 CM.   HEIGHT 15 CM.

PLATE XLI

LENGTH 475 MM.   HEIGHT 33 CM.   HEIGHT 33 CM.   LENGTH 50 CM.   HEIGHT 33 CM.

PAINTED WOODEN BOXES OF IOUIYA.

PLATE XLII

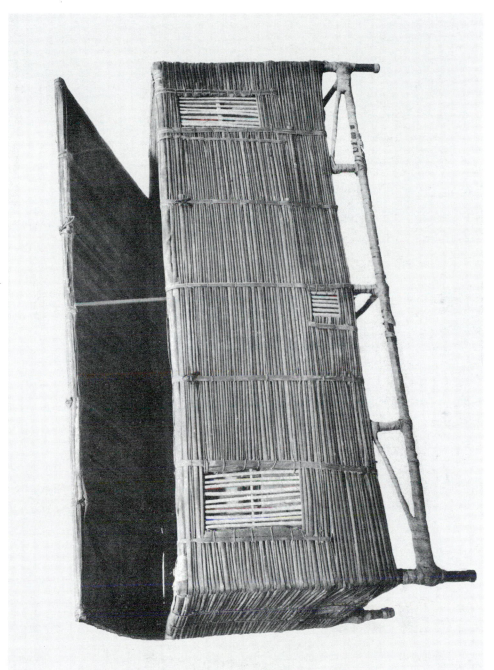

WIG-BASKET.

LENGTH 107 CMS.   HEIGHT O5O CM.

PLATE XLII.

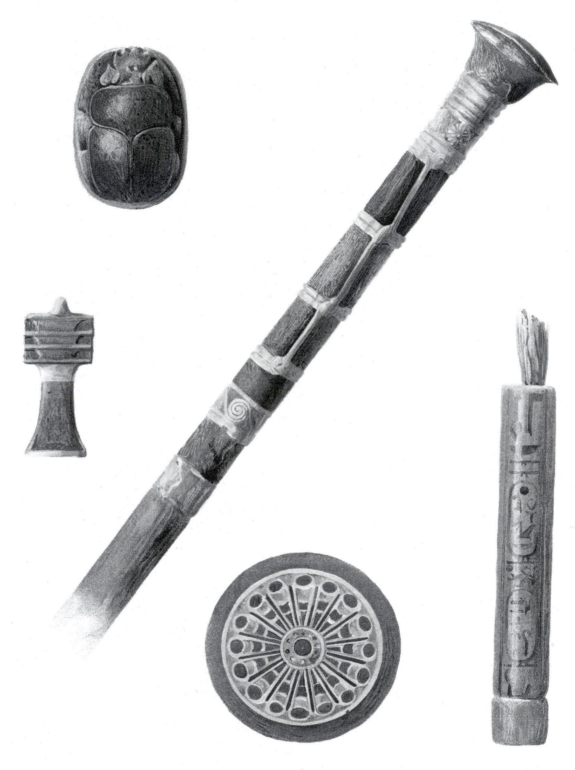

OBJECTS FROM THE TOMB OF IOUIYA.

PLATE XLIV.

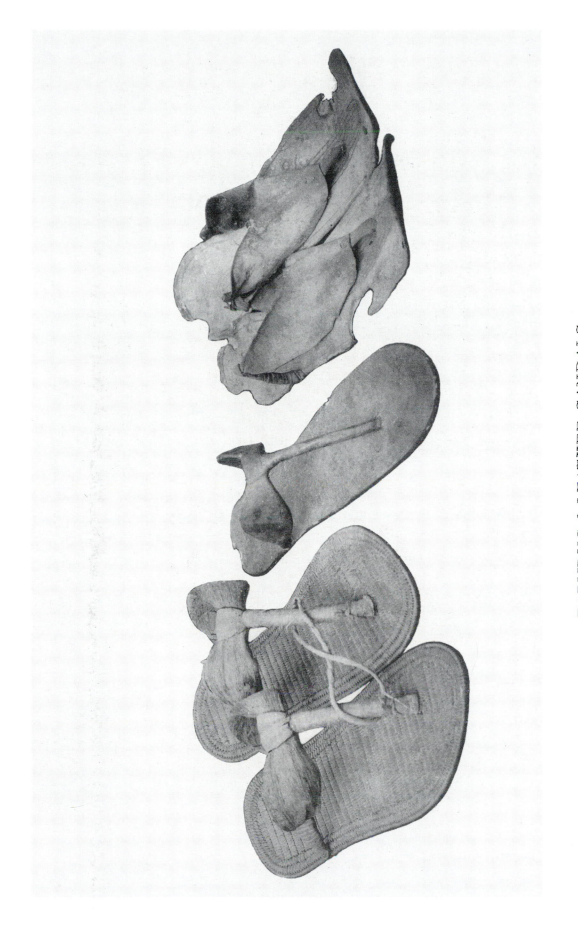

THE

FUNERAL PAPYRUS

OF

IOUIYA.

THEODORE M. DAVIS'

EXCAVATIONS: BIBÂN EL MOLÛK.

THE

FUNERAL PAPYRUS

OF

IOUIYA.

WITH AN INTRODUCTION BY

EDOUARD NAVILLE,

Hon. D.C.L., LL.D., Ph.D., Litt.D., Hon. F.S.A.,
Correspondent of the Institute of France; Foreign Member of the Hungarian Academy of Sciences;
Fellow of King's College, London.

Duckworth

CONTENTS.

PREFACE.

WHOEVER has made a study of the Book of the Dead cannot but welcome the publication of a good text of the time of the XVIIIth dynasty, for it is only by comparison of numerous documents that we shall arrive at the intelligence of this interesting and sometimes most obscure book. Therefore, we feel most thankful to Mr. Theodore M. Davis for having consented to make a special publication of the papyrus of Iouiya, which he discovered, together with all the beautiful monuments described in another book, and which is very valuable for several reasons, and particularly for its being dated. Although this volume is primarily for Egyptologists, in the introduction I have here and there put in some matter which might interest readers outside our narrow circle, to which it is not new; but I have not explained in detail the nature of the Book of the Dead; I take it as known.

In comparing this text with others published before, I was obliged to take as a basis my edition of the Book of the Dead, of the XVIIIth to XXth dynasties, quoting occasionally the Saite version first published by Lepsius. A translation has been made of the Book of the Dead by the late Sir Peter le Page Renouf, of which his premature death did not allow him to finish more than three-fourths and which I carried to its end. I generally quote this translation whenever I agree with Renouf, which is usually the case. However, I differ from this eminent scholar on one important point: the sense of the title of the book. Where Renouf reads *coming forth by day*, I translate *coming out of the day*. The day is, in my opinion, a man's life which is limited by time, also by the fact of man not being able to change his appearance; his day has a morning and evening. Coming out of the day is to be delivered from all these limits, and to be able to assume all forms one likes.

But I am quite at one with Renouf about the real sense of those chapters. They are not descriptions of what is said in their titles ; they are the magic words which bring about the result indicated by those titles ; therefore, whether we translate, chapter *whereby* one escapeth corruption, or chapter *for* escaping, or chapter *of* escaping, that does not mean any difference in the interpretation.

In order not to have constantly to repeat title, epithets, and name of Iouiya, I have used everywhere the word " the deceased."

We can only wish that future excavations may provide us with other texts of the Book of the Dead as valuable as that of Iouiya.

EDOUARD NAVILLE.

Malagny, near Geneva,
September, 1907.

DESCRIPTION OF THE PAPYRUS.

THE funeral papyrus of [hieroglyphs] is a good specimen of the Book of the Dead of the XVIIIth dynasty. We know its date. It is of the time of Amenophis III, the last king before the religious revolution of Akhouenaten.

It measures 9 metres 70 c.m. and contains forty chapters, one of which is unknown. It is written, like all the copies of the Book of the Dead of that time, in linear hieroglyphics, which are not perfect, but which are a transition towards hieratic.

The vignettes illustrating a certain number of the chapters are beautifully drawn and coloured. It certainly is a choice document, which is in accordance with the high rank of the deceased. Judging from the papyri of that epoch which have been preserved, we can see that what gave to those documents their value in the estimation of the old Egyptians, was in the first place the vignettes. It was that which they mostly cared for; the text might be more or less neglected, since probably a few only of the people who saw it could read it; besides, the scribes knew that it was to be hidden in a tomb, where only the *ka* would look at it. Generally speaking, the beauty of the vignettes runs counter to the goodness of the text; in papyri written with care and by copyists who were not mere workmen, such as those of Nebseni or Nu, in the British Museum, the vignettes, though well drawn, have no colour, they are less numerous, and are something secondary.

This papyrus is an exception in that way; though being beautifully illustrated, the text is good. Nevertheless, the parts which are inferior to the rest of the document are precisely those where there are beautiful vignettes. As they were made first, and as sufficient space had not been reserved for the text to which they belonged, there are omissions, or the chapter is sometimes curtailed.

The copying of papyri of the Book of the Dead must have been a profitable industry at the time of the XVIIIth dynasty. They were of various lengths, probably in proportion to the price paid for them. They were written

2

beforehand ; blank spaces were left in many places, chiefly at the beginning of the chapters, for the name and titles of the deceased, which were inserted only after the papyrus had been purchased. Sometimes, also, space was kept blank for a vignette which was to record some special feature of the deceased.

It is easy to see that the papyrus of Iouiya is one of those documents prepared beforehand. After the title, written in red, of each chapter, the first copyist left a blank of arbitrary length. The next writer, who had to insert the name, had not exactly the same hand, his characters are thinner and he used a different ink. As he had to adapt the name and titles to the length of the gaps, in many cases he found room only for the name ⸢hieroglyphs⸣, without any title or qualification. In other cases, on the contrary, he had to lengthen the titles as much as he could, and to add epithets, in order to fill up the space he had at his disposal. (See Pl. 20 and Pl. 21.)

We have two examples of important vignettes which recalled some of the characteristic features of the deceased, and which were made after the papyrus had been appropriated (Pl. 1 and Pl. 18). In Plate 1, which is a scene of adoration to Osiris, Iouiya is followed by his wife ; in Plate 18, where he is seen approaching the Elysian fields, he is alone. In both cases the artist wished to indicate clearly that Iouiya was a very old man when he died ; therefore he made him a quite white wig ; while, as Mr. Carter pointed out to me, grey hair is often represented by the conventional colour for grey, which is green.[1]

The titles of Iouiya are given in full on Plate 18 :—

These titles are not quite the same as those found on the furniture or on the vases in the tomb, except the two first.[2] ⸢hieroglyphs⸣, which is sometimes translated "prince" certainly indicates a rank at court ; ⸢hieroglyph⸣ I should translate "seal-bearer" or "chancellor." ⸢hieroglyphs⸣ "the only friend," seems to be very like ⸢hieroglyphs⸣, which has been found before. I do not know the real sense of the following : ⸢hieroglyphs⸣ "the great of the great ones." I should

[1] See Deir el-Bahari I, Pl. XIV, the face of Thoutmosis I.
[2] The tomb of Iouiya and Touiyou, p. xiii and ff.

translate [hieroglyphs] "the investor of friends," he who gives them the investiture of the title of "friend," he who confers this dignity upon them, [hieroglyphs] "the chief of the *rekhit.*" These men seem to have been a privileged caste; what we should call by the modern names of peers. They took part in the coronation. It is to them that the heir was presented; they were the first to pay him homage. Iouiya had been appointed their chief.

The following words are titles of courtesy, or epithets, rather than the indication of functions; but at the end comes a real title [hieroglyphs] or as we find more than twenty times [hieroglyphs] "the divine father of the lord of the two lands," which, as Dr. Borchardt has shown, means father-in-law of the king. [hieroglyphs] is often abridged in [hieroglyphs], and this qualification father-in-law of the king, or simply father-in-law, is by far the most frequent one given to the deceased. The king is his lord, though he is his son-in-law, [hieroglyphs] "the divine father who loves his lord." Twice we find this title [hieroglyphs] "the beloved priest," and once [hieroglyphs], which is also a title and which has not yet been well explained.

The name of Iouiya is often introduced by these words [hieroglyphs] "the favourite of the great god." The titles of courtesy are numerous: [hieroglyphs] "the much-beloved in the royal palace," [hieroglyphs] "who is well established in the favours of the sovereign," [hieroglyphs] "the great favourite of the sovereign," [hieroglyphs] "who goes in as a favourite and comes out beloved," [hieroglyphs] "the much-loved," [hieroglyphs] "the only wise, who loves his god."

It is to be noticed that, while on the monuments there are an unusually great number of variants of his name, the spelling of it never varies in the papyrus. It is always [hieroglyphs], which I should transliterate Iuau[1]; one single time I found [hieroglyphs] which is evidently a mis-spelling, a fault of the writer, since everywhere else he always writes [hieroglyphs]. Curiously, this spelling of the name does not occur among the numerous forms quoted from

---

[1] I have adopted M. Maspero's transcription, Iouiya, in order to preserve the uniformity with the volume on the monuments of the tomb.

the monuments by M. Maspero. The most similar form would be [hieroglyphs] where there is an [hieroglyph] at the end instead of an [hieroglyph].

Exactly the reverse occurs in the name of his wife. Unfortunately, it is destroyed in the scene at the beginning, but in the four times we see it in the picture of the Elysian fields it is written [hieroglyphs], which is the spelling on the historical scarabs of Amenophis III,[1] while M. Maspero quotes only [hieroglyphs] and [hieroglyphs]. Here it is the contrary of the former case; the monuments give an [hieroglyph] and the papyrus an [hieroglyph].

M. Maspero considers man and wife as being natives. It seems to me quite certain about the wife, looking at her type of face. If, as has been often supposed, there is a foreign element in one of them, it must be Iouiya, whose type is different from that of his wife. His very aquiline face might be Semitic; besides, the numerous transcriptions of his name seem to show that, for the Egyptians, it was a foreign sound which they reproduced in writing as they heard it; just as in our time two Egyptians will not spell alike a German, French, or English name.

As for the text itself, we have only a few remarks to make. As usual, though the signs are turned to the right, the papyrus begins on the left side, which is the East. The whole text runs from East to West, according to the symbolical march of the man's life.

The name or title of the deceased is generally introduced immediately after [hieroglyph] "said by" or [hieroglyph]. Only once Iouiya is called Osiris [hieroglyph], at the very beginning, in the first line of the first chapter. "Osiris the divine father of the sovereign, Iuau." The qualification of Osiris given to the deceased became customary only in the XIXth dynasty.

The sign of the negative [hieroglyph] exists, while in the papyri of the early part of the dynasty it is only [hieroglyph]. The sign [hieroglyph] is made exactly like [hieroglyph] as in some of the older texts. While the sign [hieroglyph] is often used for the amulet of that form, or in the word [hieroglyph], it is never found in the name of the city of Busiris which is always written [hieroglyphs]. A fact also to be noted is the frequent use of [hieroglyph] for [hieroglyph]; [hieroglyphs] for [hieroglyphs].

There are some interesting grammatical variants which cannot be noticed here.

---

[1] P. Newberry, *Scarabs*, Pl. XXXII; *id. Scarab-shaped Seals*, No. 37393; Frazer, *Egyptian Scarabs*, Pl. X; Ward, *The Sacred Beetle*, p. 64.

CONTENTS OF THE PAPYRUS.

THE papyrus of Iouiya, like all those of the Theban epoch, contains only a certain number of the chapters of the Book of the Dead. They are placed in an order very different from that which was adopted in the Saite version.

These are the chapters found in the papyrus :—1, 10, 17, 18, 30B, 63A, 64, 77, 81A, 82, 83, 84, 85, 86, 87, 99, 100 (129), 101, 102, 103, 104, 110, 117, 118, 119, 125, 136A, B, 141–3, 144, 146, 148, 149, 150, 151, 153A, 155, 156, besides an unknown chapter with the common title [hieroglyphs], and a text with rubric, found in the Saite version at the beginning of Chapter 148, and of which Dr. Budge at first made Chapter 190.

Except for a few chapters there is no fixed order ; the book must be compared to a collection of psalms. Here they are arranged in the following way :—

Plate 1.	Scene of adoration to Osiris.	
Plate 2.	Chapter 1.	
,, ,,	,, 17.	
Plates 3–5.	Chapter 17.	
Plate 6.	Chapter 17.	End.
,, ,,	,, 18.	
Plate 7.	Chapter 18.	End.
,, ,,	,, 83.	Vignette.
,, ,,	,, 84.	Vignette.
,, ,,	,, 85.	Vignette.
Plate 8.	Chapter 85.	End.
,, ,,	,, 77.	Vignette.
,, ,,	,, 86.	Vignette.
,, ,,	,, 82.	Vignette.

NOTES ON THE VARIOUS CHAPTERS.

ADORATION OF OSIRIS.

THE papyrus begins with a scene of adoration to Osiris. The god, clad in white, is sitting on his throne wearing the *atef* crown, and holding the insignia of the judge—the book and the flail. His name is much destroyed. "Osiris Khent Ament, the great god . . . . the lord of the land . . . . Unnofris, the lord of Abydos."

Before the god is a mat, covered with offerings and victuals and a bunch of blue lotus. Near the mat are three sealed vases adorned with the same flowers.

Iouiya is behind, with raised arms, adoring Osiris ; he wears a white wig, showing that he is an old man, and a broad necklace with the amulet of the heart. He has also two bracelets. The beginning only of the words has been preserved. "Adoring Osiris, kissing the ground before Unnofris. Said by the divine father (father-in-law) of the lord of the two lands, the favoured of the good god, Iouiya . . . ." He is followed by his wife wearing a long black wig made of wool, such as those which have been found repeatedly in tombs ; she has also large circular earrings, four bracelets, and she holds a sistrum and a garland of flowers.

CHAPTER 1.

The title is shorter than usual : "The day of the burial ; the arriving after going out (of the day)." The vignette shows the funeral procession. A canopy, under which lies the mummy, has been raised on a sledge drawn by attendants and by two cows, towards the door of the tomb. There stands another coffin, probably the outer one which is to contain that in which the mummy is enclosed.

Chapter 17.

As it is often the case, Chapter 17 follows Chapter 1. It is complete, in the version of the XVIIIth dynasty, which is much longer than that of the XIth, known from various tombs. If we compare this papyrus to others of the same epoch, we notice that the text is very similar to that of the papyrus which I have called *Ca*, and which is written for a controller of the cattle of Amon, called Amenophis, a Theban. There are variants with the text of the papyrus called Aa, which was written for a Memphite. Chapter 17 is one of the most important of the Book of the Dead. It begins with the cosmogony, according to the doctrine of Heliopolis.

The title is the following :—

"The beginning of the recitation of the religious formularies, when going out and coming back to the Underworld, being glorified in the good Ament, being among the followers of Osiris, being satisfied with the victuals of Unnofris ; of going out of the day and taking all the forms which one desires to assume ; of playing draughts when sitting in the pavilion ; of the appearing as a living spirit, of the deceased, after he has gone to his rest. This is the magic virtue of him who reads it on earth."

Chapter 17 is the only one in which a kind of commentary is introduced by the words : "What is that ? " Variants, other readings, are also quoted after the words : " or else." The chapter begins thus :—

"These are the words of the Lord Tûm. I am Tûm when I am the only one, I am Nu, I am Ra when he rises, when he first began to be ruler. What is that ? Ra, who first began to be ruler, is Ra when he rose as a king, when there was yet no firmament, and when he stood on the height of Amshmûn.

"I am the great god born by himself. Who is that ? Ra, born by himself, is water, is Nu, the father of the gods, or else Ra who created his names, the lord of the cycle of the gods. What is it ? Ra, when he created the names of his limbs, these became the gods around him ; the god whom nobody opposes. Who is that ? Tûm in his solar disk, or else Ra when he rises on the eastern horizon of the sky.

"I am yesterday (the past) and I know the morrow. What is that ? Yesterday is Osiris, and the morrow is Ra,[1] on the day when he destroyed the enemies of the Lord of the Universe, and he made a ruler of his son Horus."

---

[1] Osiris, the god who dies and is buried, is the symbol of the past ; while Ra, who rises under the form of Horus, is that of the future.

CHAPTER 18.

Is as usual without a title. It generally follows immediately Chapter 17. It is a litany to Thoth beseeching the god to make the deceased triumphant over his enemies in various places.

It ends with the following rubric: "If a man reads this sacred chapter he comes out of the day after he has gone to his rest. He takes all the forms he chooses. Also, whoever has this book recited over him every day, he will be prosperous upon earth, he will come forth safe from every fire, and no evil thing will approach him, regularly, for times infinite."

The Theban papyri add to this rubric these words, which are obscure: "What I shall see will be in abundance." I believe this refers to the creative power of the eye. Whatever I have seen with my own eyes represented in any way, or whatever is pictured to my fancy, will be, will exist. The texts add [hieroglyphs], which I should translate, "in my hand," or "in my possession."

CHAPTERS OF THE TRANSFORMATIONS.

Here begins a series of eight chapters, those of the transformations, which all have the same title: [hieroglyphs], "assuming the form of." There are usually nine, very rarely eleven. They are not always in the same order. That of the Saite version is very different from that of the Theban; besides they are much more scattered than they are here. This papyrus has only eight; it omits Chapter 78, which is the longest. They are in the following order, which is the most usual: Chapters 83, 84, 85, 77, 86, 82, 87, 81. They all have very well drawn vignettes which allow one to recognize the animals.

Chapter 83. "Assuming the form of a Bennû," which has sometimes been considered as the phœnix, and which M. Loret determines as a heron.

Chapter 84. "Assuming the form of a Hernshaw" (Renouf). It is shorter than usual; the vignette having been made beforehand, insufficient space had been left for the text. It begins, line 3 [hieroglyphs], and the last line also is incomplete.

Chapter 85. "Assuming the form of a living soul, in order not to come into the dungeon, and not to perish eternally." The soul has been the form of a bird with a human head. Many papyri have a ram instead, which reads also *ba*. This chapter is much abridged at the end.

Chapter 77. "Assuming the form of a golden hawk," or according to M. Loret, of a golden falcon.

Chapter 86. "Assuming the form of a swallow," which is on the vignette. Sometimes the bird looks more like a dove. This chapter has a rubric: "He who knows this chapter, he returns after going out of the day, in all forms he likes in the field of Aarru."

Chapter 82. "Assuming the form of Phtah, eating bread, drinking beer, easing oneself, and living at On." The vignette represents the god of Memphis.

Chapter 87. "Assuming the form of a serpent." A very short chapter, as is also the following.

Chapter 81. "Assuming the form of a lotus." The lotus here represented is the blue lotus.

CHAPTER 63A.

There are two versions of this chapter in the Theban papyri. This is what I have called 63A. The vignette represents a man drinking water, which flows out of a tree called in other texts "the sycamore of Nut." The title is here: "Chapter of drinking water."

CHAPTER 64.

It is by no means uncommon in the Theban papyri to find two versions of Chapter 64; one of them being a kind of summary or abridgment of the whole book. This short version has a peculiar title, which we find here incorrectly reproduced: "Chapter of knowing all the chapters of (the book) going out of the day, in one chapter."

This has a curious rubric showing that it was customary with the ancient Egyptians to put books in foundation walls. "This chapter was found in the foundations of Amhunnû (the temple of Heliopolis) by an overseer of masons, in the time of the King of Upper and Lower Egypt, Septi. Mysterious figures which nobody had seen nor looked at." These last words evidently mean that the book was written in old character, which were no longer understood at the time of the discovery.

CHAPTERS 141–143.

"The book said by a man, or his father, or his son, in the festival of the Ament, wherewith he becomes the favorite of Ra, and of the gods when he is with them; said on the day of the new moon."

This chapter which is divided into three in the Saite version, is a long series of names of gods or genii, and the list of all the places where Osiris is worshipped. Amon and the gods of Thebes do not appear among these names.

At the end of the chapter is a long title and rubric which in the late papyri is the beginning of Chapter 148. In the early ones it introduces one of the hymns to the setting sun which is part of Chapter 15.

CHAPTER 104.

"Chapter of sitting in the midst of the great gods." The vignette represents the deceased before three gods.

CHAPTER 103.

"Chapter of being near Hathor." Very short; has no vignette.

CHAPTER 10 OR 48.

"Chapter for coming forth against one's enemies." In the Saite version, this chapter appears twice at different places. Here it has a most interesting vignette which, at present, is unique. The deceased drives a lance into the neck of an enemy bound by the elbows.

CHAPTER 118.

"Chapter of arriving at Ro-setu." The vignettes in this chapter and in the next represent the deceased in front of something which looks like a sarcophagus, but which in the monuments of the first dynasties means a hut.

CHAPTER 117.

"Chapter of taking the path to Ro-setu." In several of the old papyri the deceased, with a cane in his hand, is seen climbing a mountain.

CHAPTER 119.

"Chapter of going out of Ro-setu," which is represented here as a door.

CHAPTER 148.

"Chapter of giving sustenance to the deceased, in the Netherworld, granting that his soul be on earth, living eternally, no evil things will prevail in him." This chapter gives the names of the seven celestial cows, with the bull, which are all represented here, each one before an altar.

The rubric gives an idea of the magic effect of the book. "(The book called) giving sustenance to the deceased in the Netherworld delivers a man from all evil things. Thou shalt not read it to any other man than thyself, this the book of Unnefer. He to whom this book has been read, Ra is his steersman and his protecting power, in the Netherworld, in the sky and on earth, in all places where he goes, without intermittence."

CHAPTER 151.

This is the text only of a chapter in which the vignettes are generally the prominent part. Here they are totally absent. The chapter describes an ideal funerary chamber, which is supposed to be built and adorned exactly according to the prescriptions of the book of the *Tuat*, the Underworld. Therefore the title is: "Hidden writings of the Tuat." These writings are also the words which are said over the various amulets or objects in the chamber, or by the gods or genii.

When there is a representation of the chamber we see in the middle a canopy. Under it lies the mummy over which Anubis says certain words not found here. The chapter is very incomplete. It contains only the words referring to the objects belonging to the four walls of the chamber, and which were each placed in a little niche cut in the wall. The words also were engraved on a brick inserted in the wall, underneath the object. These objects were an ushebti figure on the North, a torch of reeds on the South, an Anubis on the East, and a Tat on the West.

The chapter begins with the magic words said over the ushebti, after which comes the rubric: "This chapter is said on a brick of green clay, it is engraved on it, and a niche is made for it in the wall of the Tuat, where also is put a figure of palm-wood seven fingers in height; its mouth is opened (it has to undergo the ceremony of the opening of the mouth); it is fastened on the brick in the Northern wall, looking towards the South." The objects of the three other walls and the magical words said on them, come each in turn. This is all we have of Chapter 151.

CHAPTER 156.

"Chapter of the buckle of carnelian given to the deceased." I have translated "carnelian"; it may be red jasper. It must be red since it represents the blood of Isis. This amulet is put on the neck of the deceased.

CHAPTER 155.

"Chapter of the Tat of gold put on the neck of the deceased." This sign represents the backbone and ribs of Osiris. Buckle and Tat are often taken as symbols of Isis and Osiris. This is the reason why these two signs are so often used as ornaments, especially on shrines.

CHAPTER 101.

This chapter has only been found once before in an old papyrus, that of Nu, in the British Museum.[1] It has a title which occurs here for the first time: "The book of binding with words for the mouth of those who are delivered from the coffin; they are put on the neck of the deceased. They do not appear in the back house, they are not known by common people. No eye has seen them, and no ear has heard them."

These somewhat obscure words are explained by the rubric, which says that these words "are on a strip of papyrus written in colour made with fruits of tamarisk mixed with incense." The meaning of the first words "binding with words" is therefore putting a bandage covered with words on the neck of the deceased. As for the following: "for the mouth of those who are delivered from their coffins," it refers to the magic effect of this chapter, which is a complete resurrection. "Whoever has these bandages (phylacteries, Renouf) put on his neck, all the favours are granted to him as to the cycle of the gods; he is united to the followers of Horus, he is established before Sothis, his body is like a god with all his attendants for ever. The goddess Menkit causes vegetation to rise out of his body. These things have been done as thy safeguard for going out of the day every day in the Ament; the Majesty of Thoth has done them, to the Majesty of King Osiris the victorious, wishing that light might shine on his body (for ever)." The last lines of the rubric are evidently incorrect. Words have been omitted which I had to supplement from the papyrus of Nu or from the Saite version. It is in the papyrus of Nu that Osiris is mentioned as a dead king.

CHAPTER 153A.

"Chapter of coming out of the net which is in the valley." The vignette is unusual. The soul of the deceased comes out of the net, and Anubis in the form of a man stretches forth his hand towards the soul. The title also

---

[1] Budge, *The Book of the Dead*, Text p. 212.

is curious. We do not understand what is a net in a valley or a mountain, when the text speaks of fishermen and water.

This very difficult chapter, which is probably compiled from two different versions, has in our text even more repetitions than in other contemporary documents.

CHAPTER 64.

This is the long version of Chapter 64, "The chapter of coming out of the day." The deceased is seen coming out of the door of his tomb. This chapter has a historical rubric similar to that of the abridged version, which we found before. It shows that this text was deposited under the feet of a statue. "This chapter was found at Eshmûn (Hermopolis) on a brick of alabaster, engraved in pure lapis, under the feet of this god (Thoth) in the time of the King of Upper and Lower Egypt, Menkaura, by the royal son Hortutef. It was found when he moved about to inspect the temples"— here come a few obscure words, which I suppose mean that someone who was with him explained or translated it to him—"He brought it to the king as a marvel, when he saw that it was something very mysterious which nobody had seen or looked at. He who reads this book must be pure, and not eat goat's flesh or fishes."

Curiously, this chapter is not complete. Suddenly we find the sign ◻, which means "gap," there is a short blank space underneath, and the whole text from line 26 to 47 of the basis taken in Aa, is entirely omitted. Evidently the original from which the writer copied was imperfect.

CHAPTER 30B.

Just as in the papyrus of Nu and also in the Saite version, immediately after Chapter 64, a rubric says that a scarab of hard stone—which is here probably jasper—encircled with gold, is to be put in the heart of the deceased. On this scarab, which is represented in the vignette, is to be engraved one of the chapters of the heart, which I have numbered 30B.

CHAPTER 110.

This chapter, often called that of the Elysian fields, has here the same title as in a London papyrus: "The arrival at the house of the Nile the abundant provider." It consists of a long text divided into various fragments, and ending with a representation of the fields or the islands of Aarru, which are called also the fields of Hotepit, of rest or felicity. Just before that picture we see Iouiya alone, with a cane in his hand; two attendants make offerings to him. One of them holding a long jug, out of which he pours water, is said to go around him four times: this jug is made of silver; the other one brings him a tray with several of the conventional signs which we know to mean cloth, material for making garments.

Like the scene at the beginning of the papyrus, this was not made beforehand. Iouiya is painted as an old man, with a white wig. A great many of his titles have been inscribed over his head. While if we look at the picture of the fields all the figures have been made beforehand. The deceased is often followed by his wife; she has black hair. The names have been added when the papyrus was appropriated.

Unknown Chapter.

"Chapter of coming out of the day." This chapter has not been found before. It is a kind of commentary to the vignette which represents nine large serpents. I believe it may be considered as an introduction to the two following chapters, for it certainly belongs to the group of the chapters of the gates and the pylons, where the deceased has to show his knowledge of the names of the occupants, the warders and the heralds. Very often, for instance, in the representations in the tombs of the kings, a large serpent is the guard of the gate. It is probably the same here. The chapter begins in this way :—

"Hail to thee, the great god who is in this lake. I know thee, I know thy name. Deliver me from these serpents which are in Ro-setu, who live on the faces (read the hearts) of men, and who eat their blood. For I know your names (the deceased addresses the serpents). Nasti (?) who lives on his neighbour, is the name of one; he whose face is turned round, is the name of another"; and so on till the seventh, although there are nine represented in the vignette. The fact of there being only seven named, would connect this chapter more intimately with the seven gates which follow. The words which come after the names of the serpents are sentences which seem rather disconnected. Probably want of space has obliged the writer to abridge them and to break off in the middle of one.

Chapter 144.

Without title and introduction. It is the chapter of the seven gates. The text consists only of three names, that of the occupant, that of the warder, and that of the herald. This very brief form of the chapter is unusual in the old papyri, except the papyrus of Nu.

Above is the representation of the gates, and below, two gods who are the warder and the herald.

CHAPTER 146.

"The beginning of the mysterious cells in the house of Osiris, in the field of Aarru." The word which Renouf translated "pylon," I should rather interpret by "cell," since we see there a genius sitting in it. There are only twelve cells here, while there are generally twenty-one. The text consists of nothing but names, that of the cell and that of the doorkeeper. This is the only place in this papyrus where the titles, or rather the epithets, given to Iouiya constantly vary; there is a different one at each cell.

Quite at the end, there are a few words of a different character: "I am Min Horus who restores Osiris, the heir to his father. I come, I give life to my father Osiris; he conquers all his enemies. I come every day from the Southern sky, and I bring Mat to her father."

THE PSYCHOSTASIA.

Under the end of Chapter 146 there is a representation which we should rather expect to find further, the weighing of the soul. It is here in its simplest form. On one side the judge, Osiris, is standing. Before him is the balance, in one scale of which is the deceased's heart; in the other, what should be the goddess Maat or her emblem; but there is something which looks like a weight, and which perhaps is unfinished. Then comes the deceased, who puts his hand on the place from which his heart has been removed; behind him is Thoth, "the lord of divine words," in the form of a cynocephalus wearing on his head the lunar disk; lastly, "Maat, the daughter of Ra."

This interesting scene is seldom so much abridged as it is here.

CHAPTER 99.

"Chapter of sailing a ship in the Netherworld." A long chapter, in which the deceased has also to show his knowledge, since every part of the ship asks to be told its mystical name. The vignette represents a sailing-boat in which the deceased is seen twice, rowing the boat and sitting on the bow. The long rubric makes the usual promises of plentiful victuals in the field of Aarru to him who knows this book.

4

Chapter 125.

The various parts which form this chapter are all found in this papyrus, and very complete. Only the weighing of the soul, which we met before, is not at its proper place.

The first part is the arrival of the deceased in the hall in which he is to be iudged. We see him with his two hands raised in the attitude of prayer. This vignette is made beforehand ; it has nothing typical of Iouiya, whose hair is painted black. The title of this introduction is here : " Words said on arriving into the hall of Righteousness, in order to see the faces of the gods " ("the divine countenances," Renouf). These words are a preliminary confession which, like the following, has the character of an apology since it is negative : " I am not a doer of wrong to men, I am not one who slayeth his kindred," and so forth.

Then should come the Psychostasia. In many papyri, the deceased is seen taken by the hand by the god Anubis, who leads him to the hall where sits Osiris.

The deceased then calls on each of the forty-two witnesses and bids each of them to testify that he has not committed one special sin : " O thou of long strides, who makest thine appearance in An, I am not a doer of wrong. O thou who holdest the fire and makest thine appearance in Kher-aha, I am not a man of violence. O thou of the long nose, who makest thine appearance at Eshmûn, I have not been evil-minded . . . ." The vignette represents a shrine enclosing the forty-two gods, each of them has a man's head and a beard ; they are all alike.

When the confession has been made, when the heart has been weighed and Osiris has declared to the deceased that he is justified, the deceased goes out of the hall. The long chapter which follows, and which here has no title, generally has one of this kind : " Words said after the hall of righteousness." At the end is a rubric of the usual kind.

Here, as in the old papyri, we find a vignette representing a pond, at the corners of which sit four apes in front of whom are flames. It is only seldom that with this vignette are words which are a prayer to the four apes that the deceased may enter the Ament, to which they answer : " come, there is no more evil in thee." In the Saite version this is Chapter 126.

Chapter 100 or 129.

This chapter often occurs two or even three times in the same papyrus : " Chapter of distinguishing the deceased, of making him to embark in the boat of Ra together with those who are with the god." The vignette represents the boat of Ra, in which stands the god, in the form of Khepera. Before him are Isis and Thoth; behind him Shu and the deceased. The words on the vignette say that a Tat and buckle are to be fastened on the deceased, so that he may navigate with Ra wherever he likes.

This chapter is part of a series of three which are generally at the end of the papyri.

Chapter 102.

"Chapter of embarking in the boat of Ra." No vignette.

Chapter 136a.

"Chapter of being conveyed in the boat of Ra." Very short chapter without vignette.

Chapter 136b.

This chapter does not exist in this form in the Saite version; but it is very frequent in the Theban papyri, where it is always the last but one of the chapters of the book: "Chapter whereby one is conveyed in the boat of Ra . . . said by the deceased in order that he may pass through the orbit of flame." The vignette represents the boat of Ra; the god is seen there as a hawk's head bearing a disk, and there is an eye at both ends of the boat. It does not navigate on water but on the sky, with numerous stars.

Chapter 149.

The usual end of the papyri of the Theban period. It is the chapter of the fourteen domains which the deceased has to reach, and in which he enjoys special privileges. The word "domain" is Renouf's translation. I should prefer "residence" or "habitation." Each of them is an enclosed space which has its inhabitants described or mentioned in the text. The deceased calls on the domain and often in the same breath goes over to the inhabitants, without any transition. The vignettes show the form and the occupants of those residences.

The proof that it is the end of the book is the rubric in the two last lines of the papyrus. Here it is much longer than usual. "This is the end (of the book); it is from beginning to end such as it was found written; it was drawn, checked, examined, weighed from part to part." Evidently, the writer wishes to show that his text is reliable.

CHAPTER 150.

Is not a special chapter.   It is only the collection of vignettes representing the fourteen domains of the preceding chapter.   Curiously, the number is not exactly the same.   There are fifteen, the fifth being replaced by two which do not agree with the description in the text.   The four serpents are probably the cardinal points.

PLATE I.

ADORATION TO OSIRIS.

PLATE II

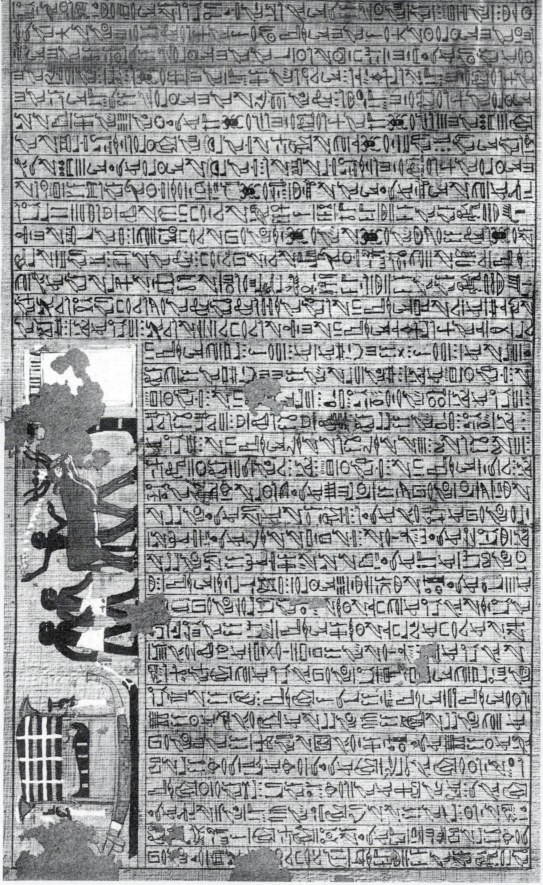

PLATE III.

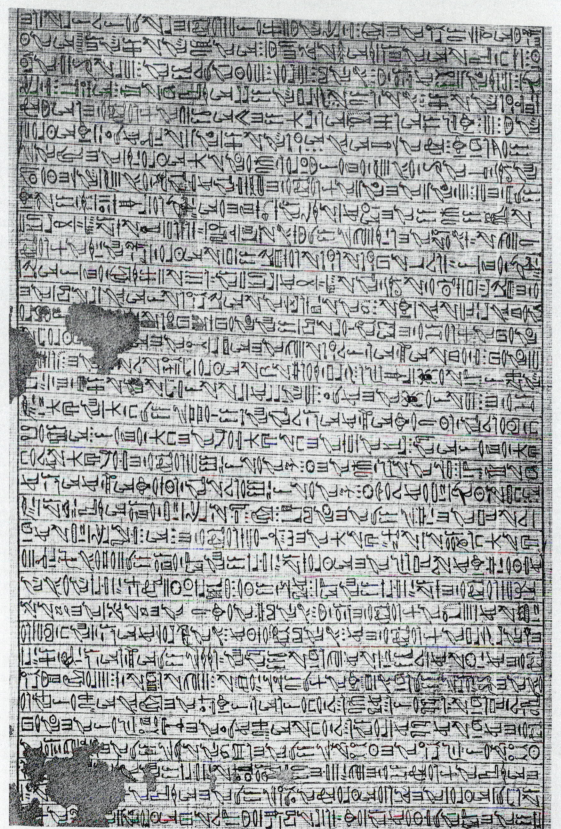

PLATE IV

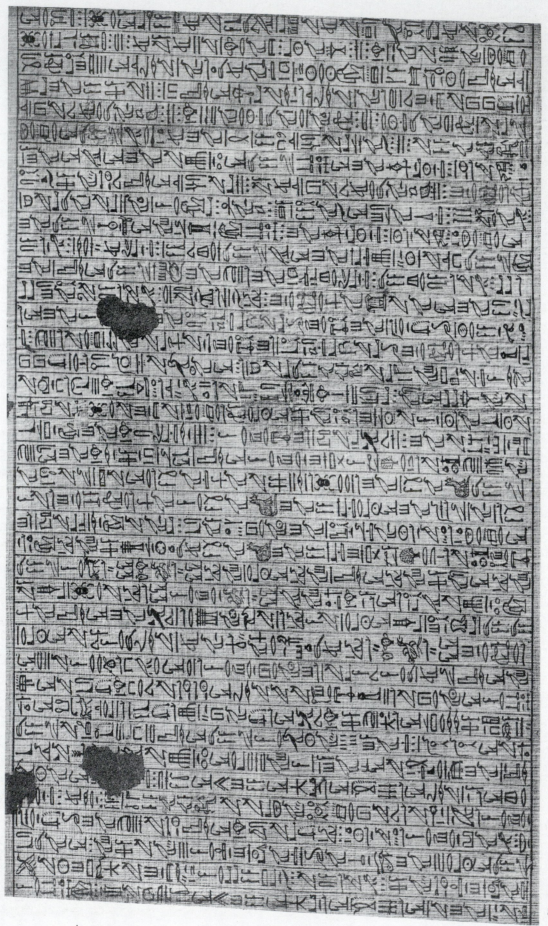

PLATE V.

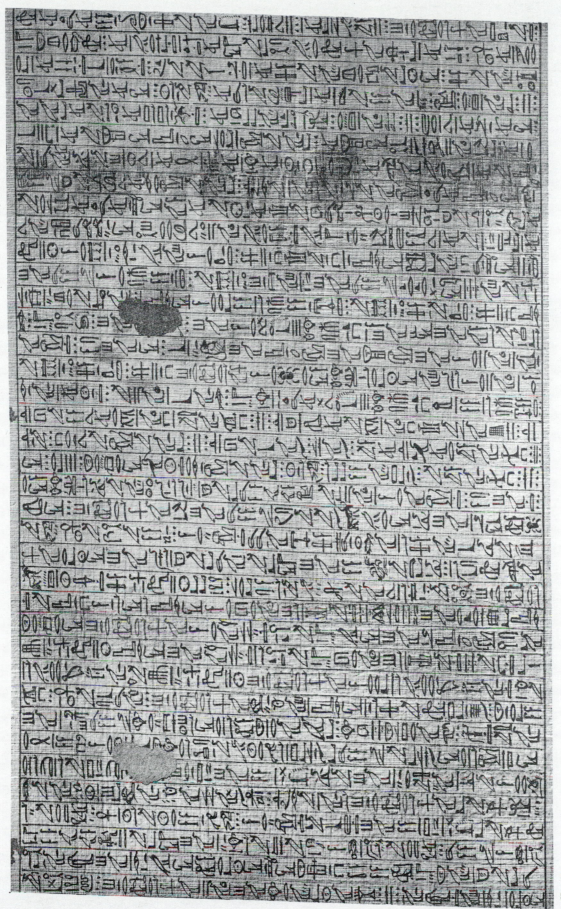

PLATE V

PLATE VII.

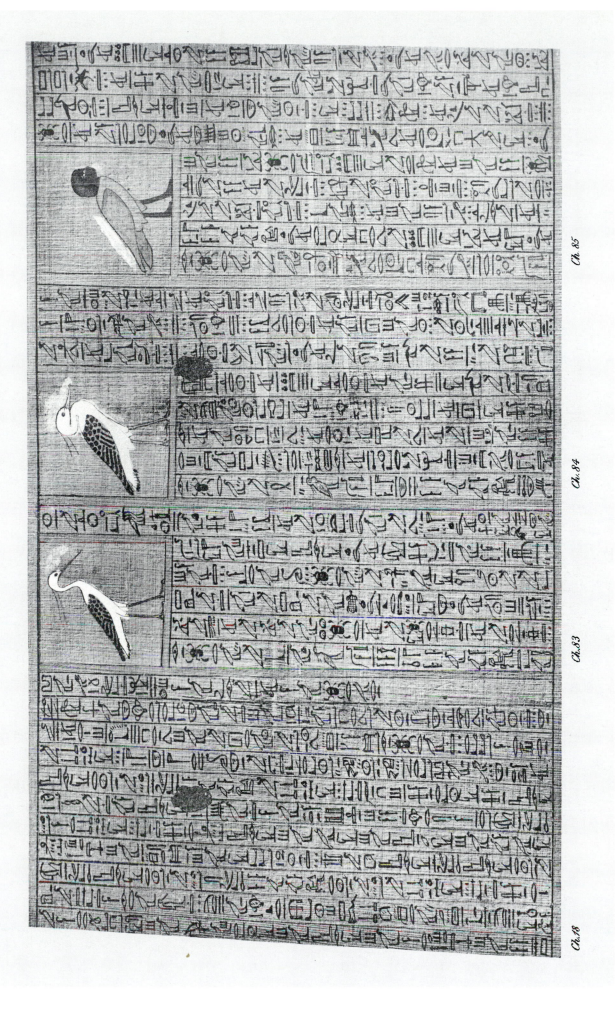

Ch. 85

Ch. 84

Ch. 83

Ch. 18

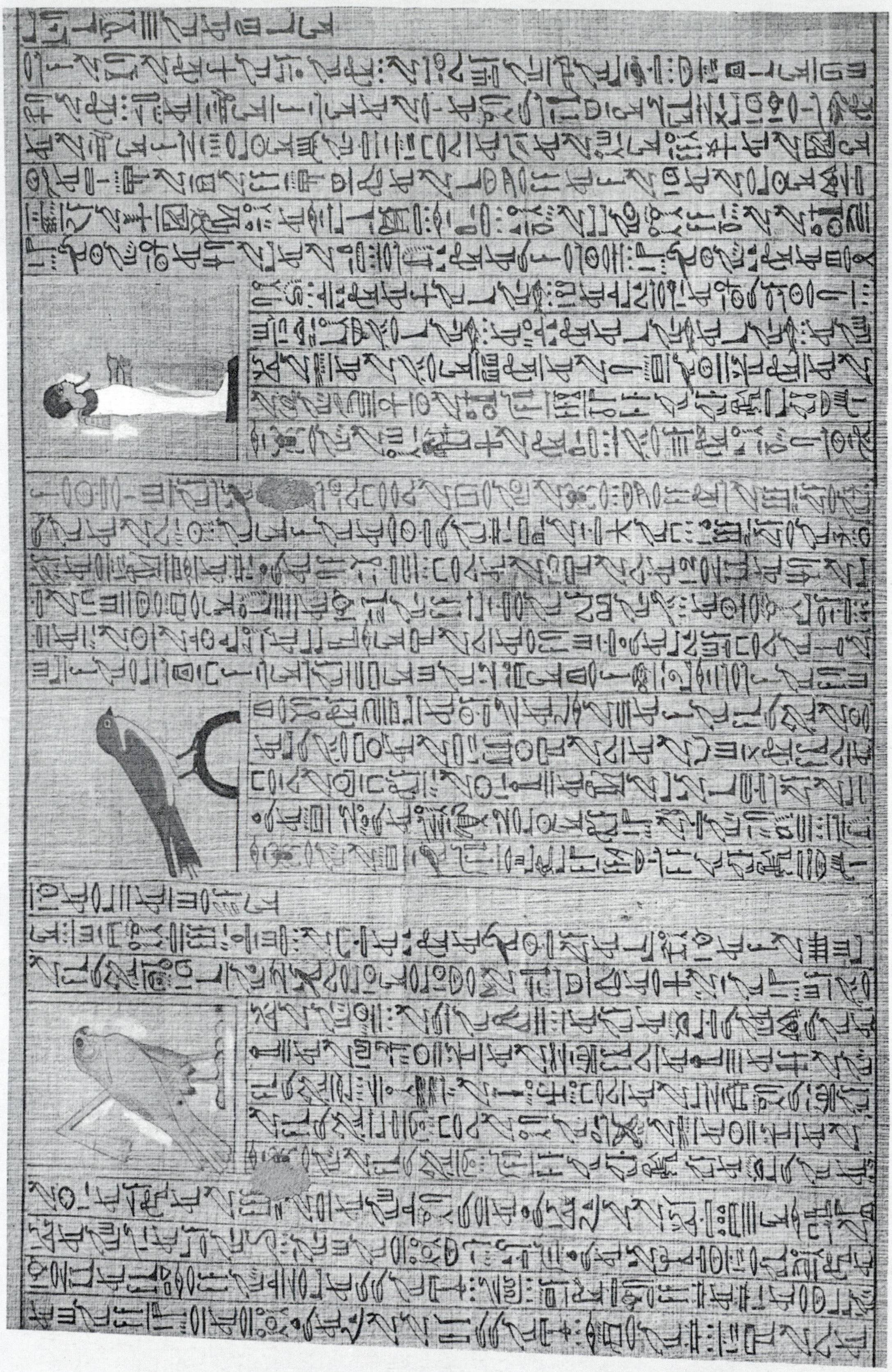

PLATE VI

Ch.82

Ch.86

Ch.77

Ch.85

PLATE IX.

Ch. 141-3

Ch. 64

Ch. 63 A

Ch. 81

Ch. 87

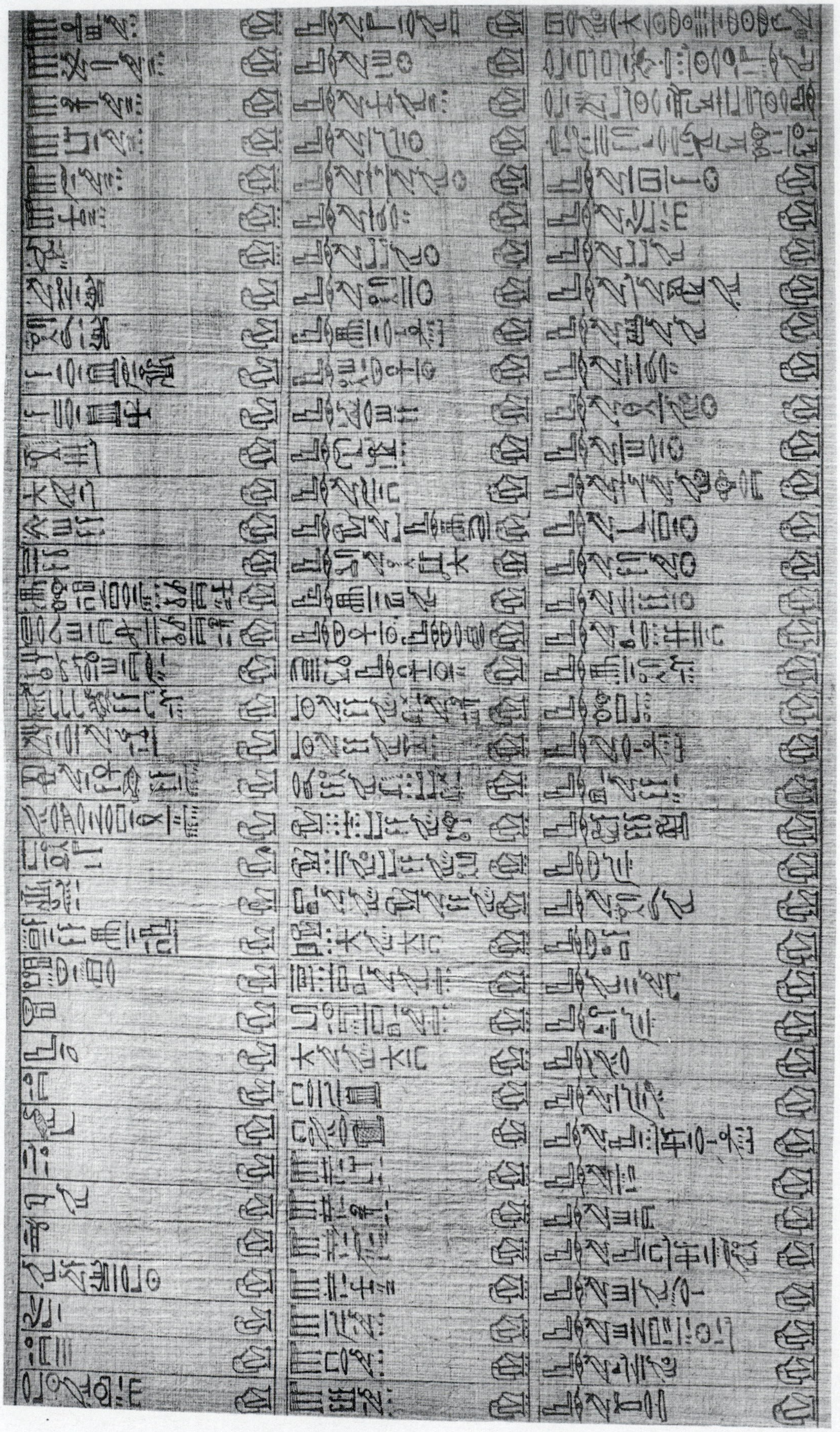

Ch. 148

Ch. 141-3

PLATE XI.

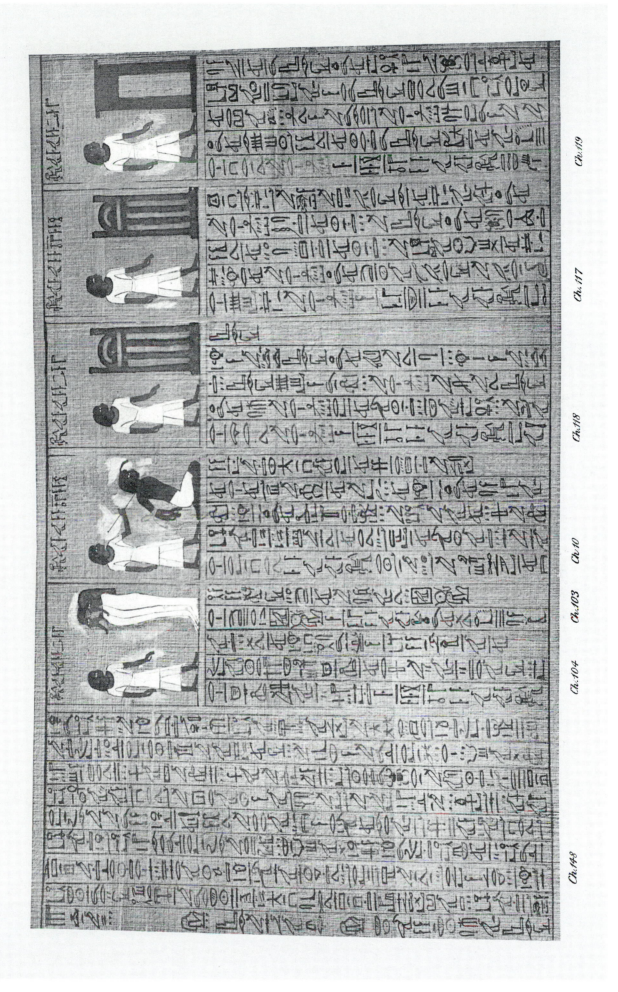

PLATE X

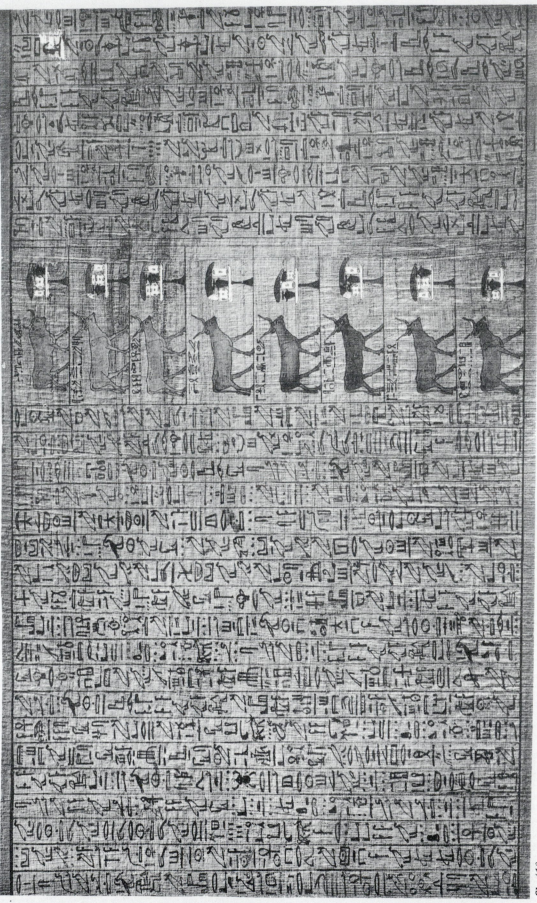

PLATE XIII.

PLATE XI

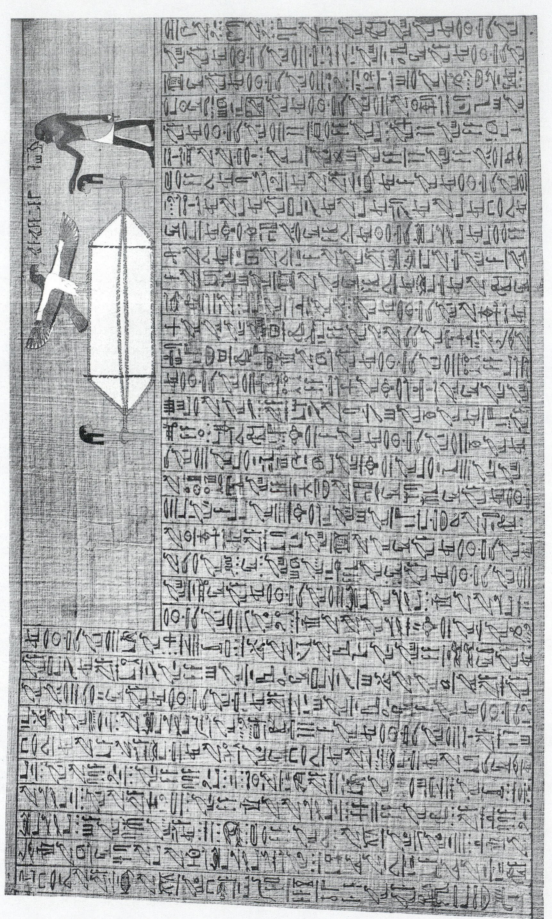

PLATE XV.

Ch. 64

Ch. 153 A

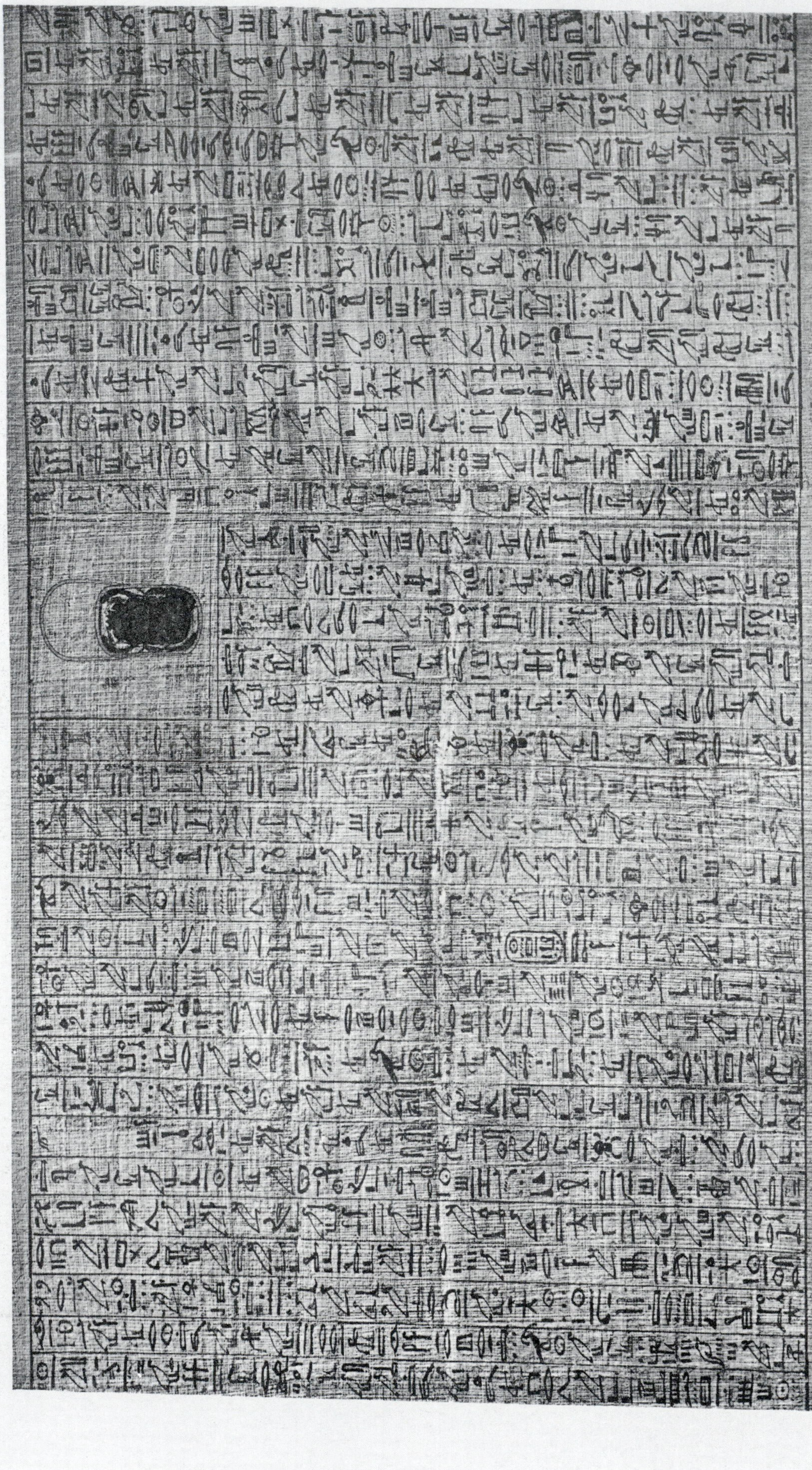

PLATE XV

PLATE XVII.

Ch. 110

PLATE XVII

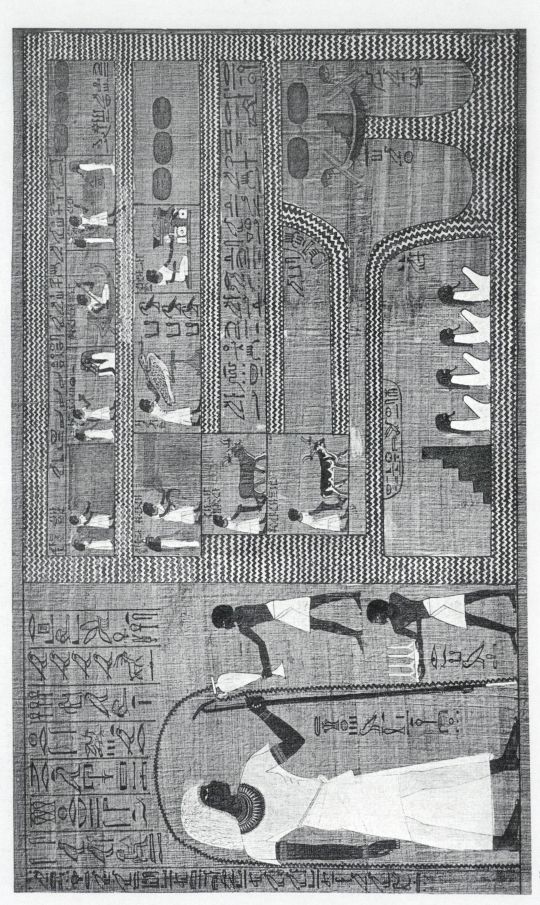

Ch. 110

PLATE XIX.

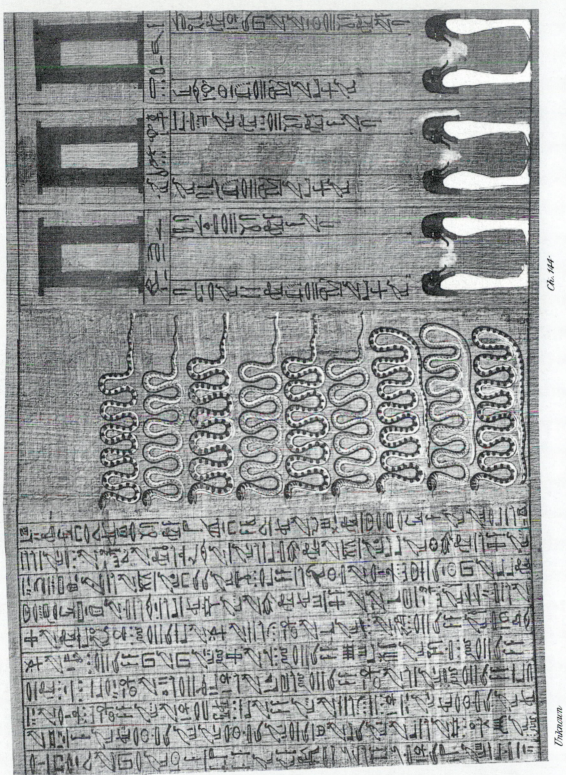

Ch. 144.

Unknown.

PLATE XX

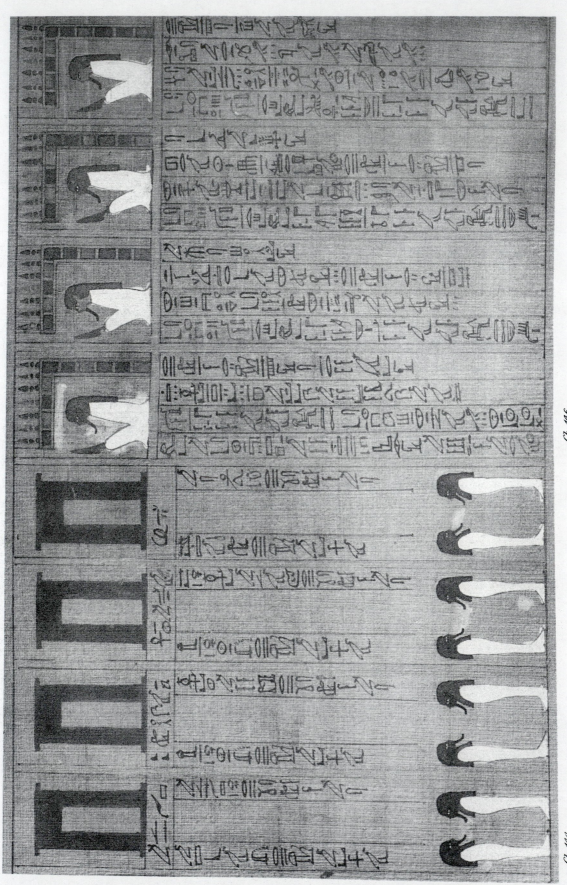

Ch. 146

Ch. 144

PLATE XXI.

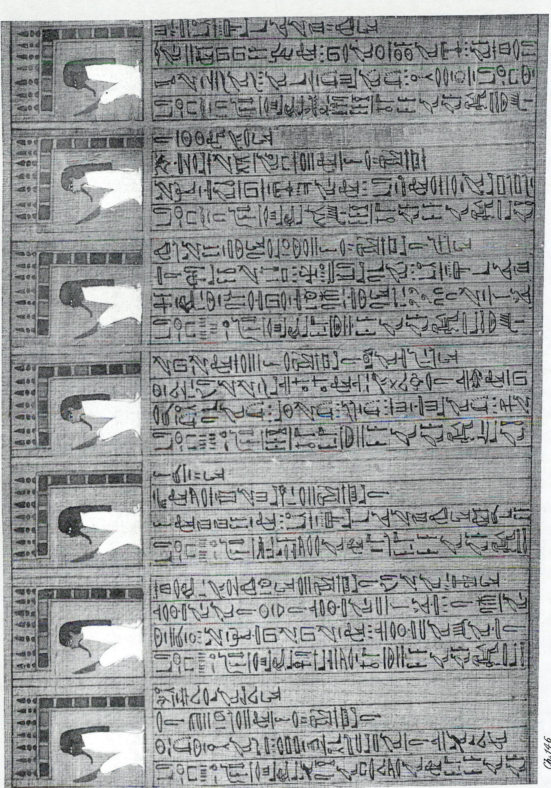

Ch.146

PLATE XXI

Ch. 99

Ch. 125

Ch. 146

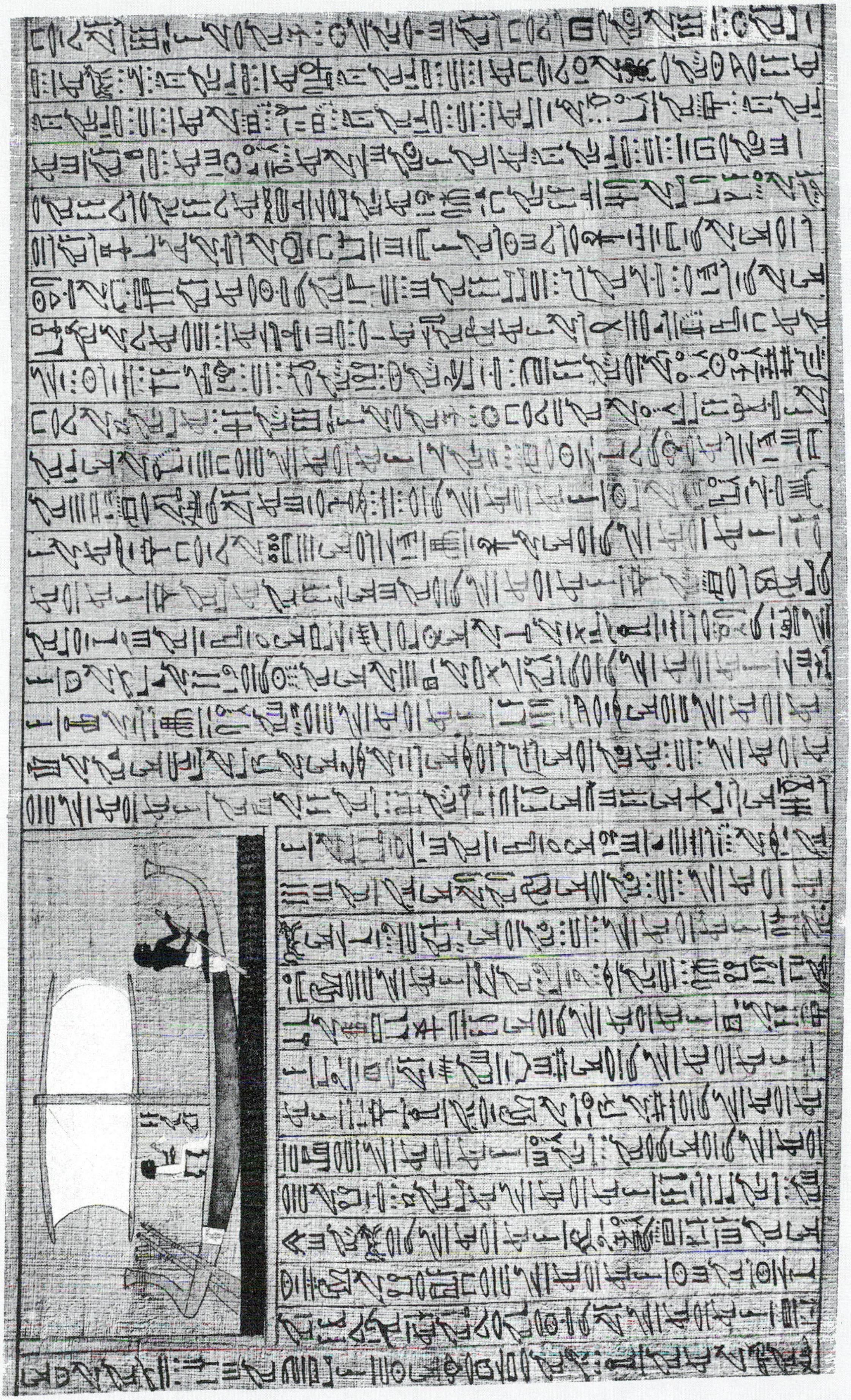

Ch. 99

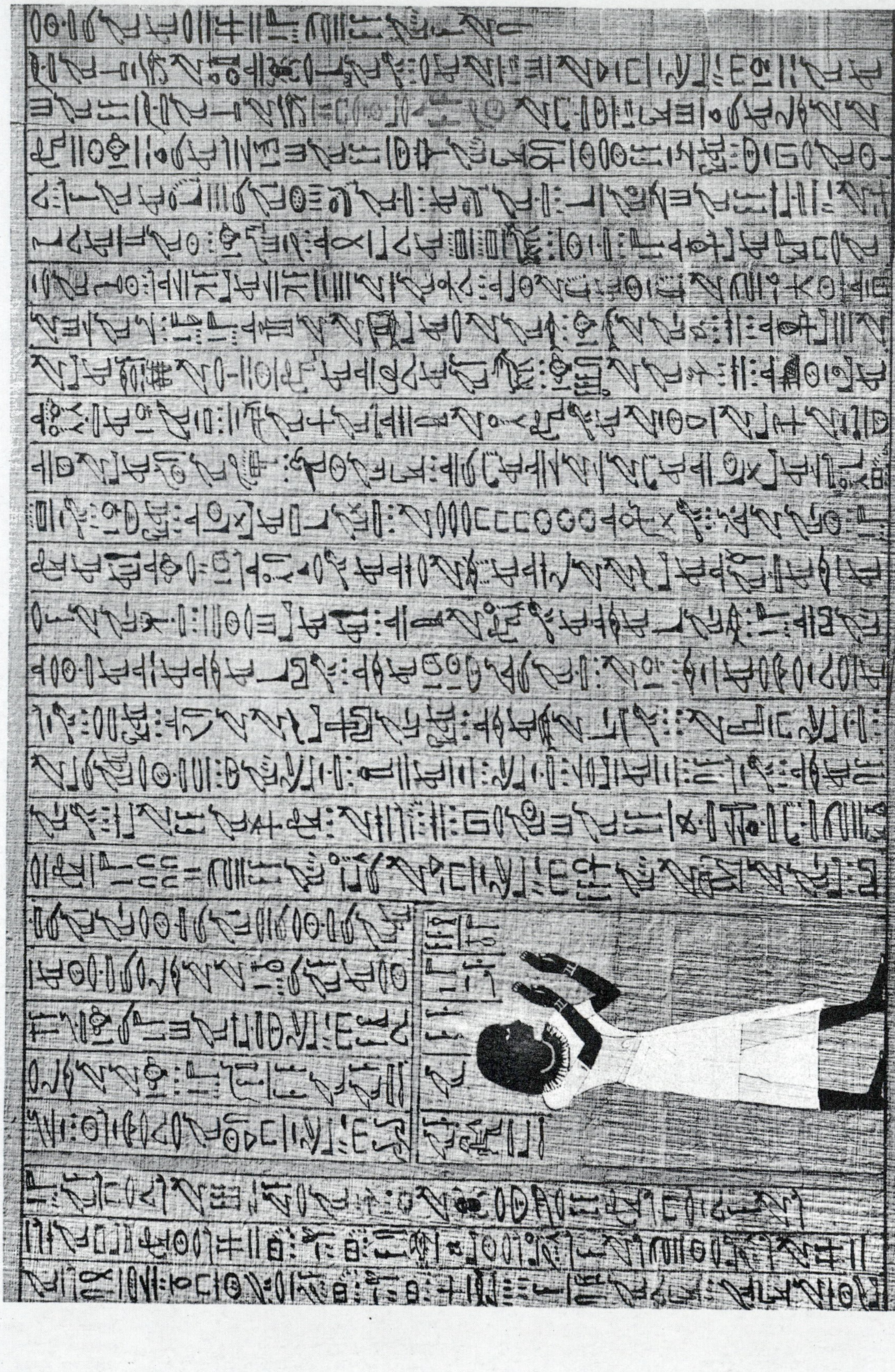

Ch. 125

Ch. 99

PLATE XXV.

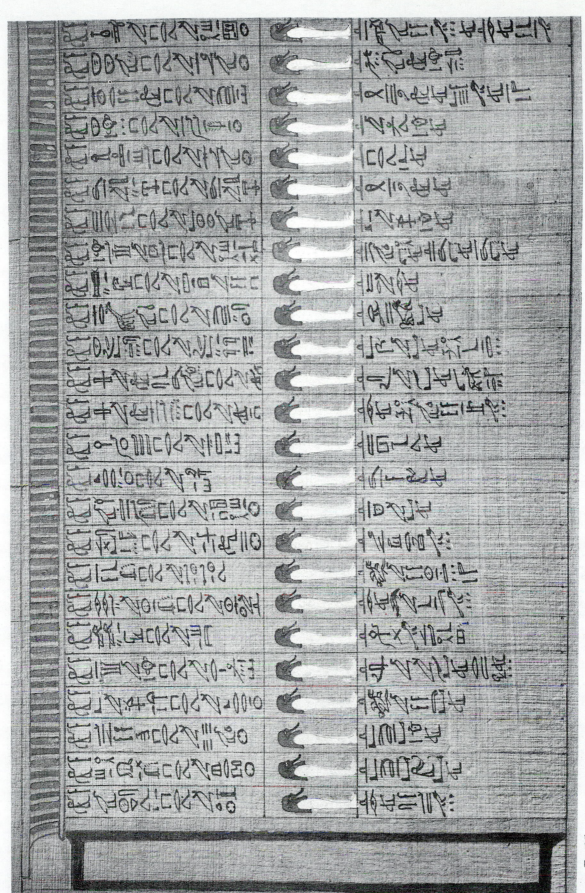

Ch. 125

PLATE XXVI

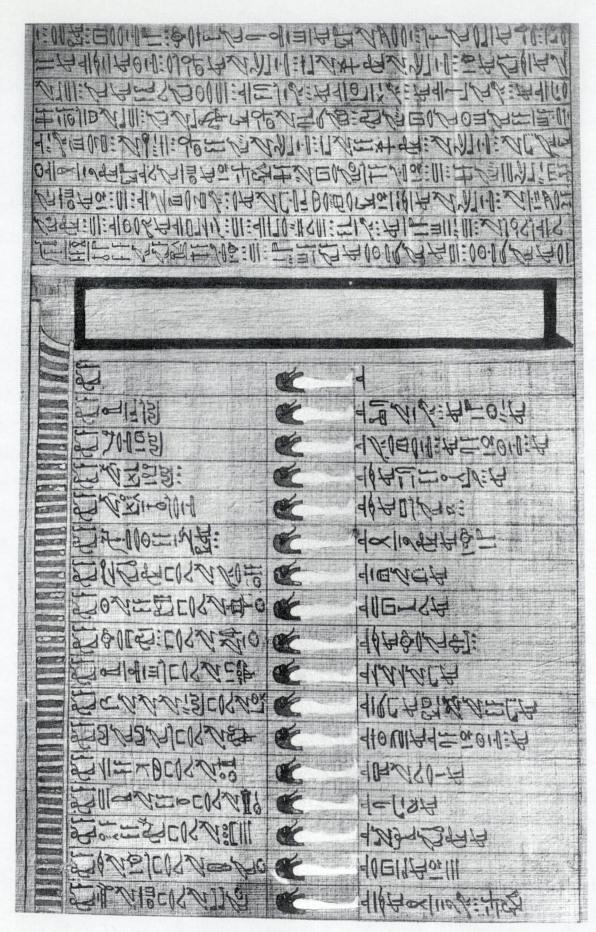

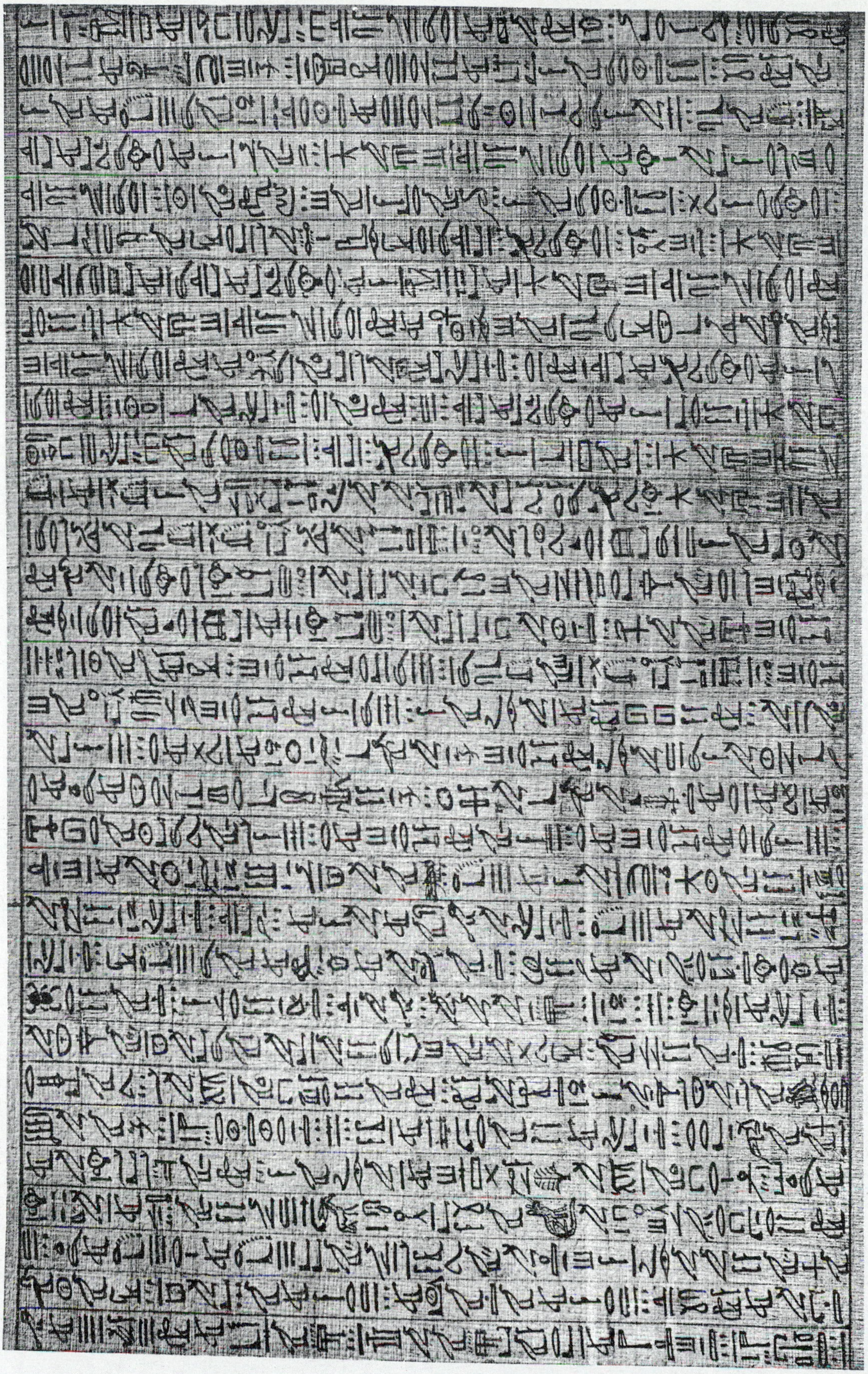

Ch. 125

PLATE XXVIII

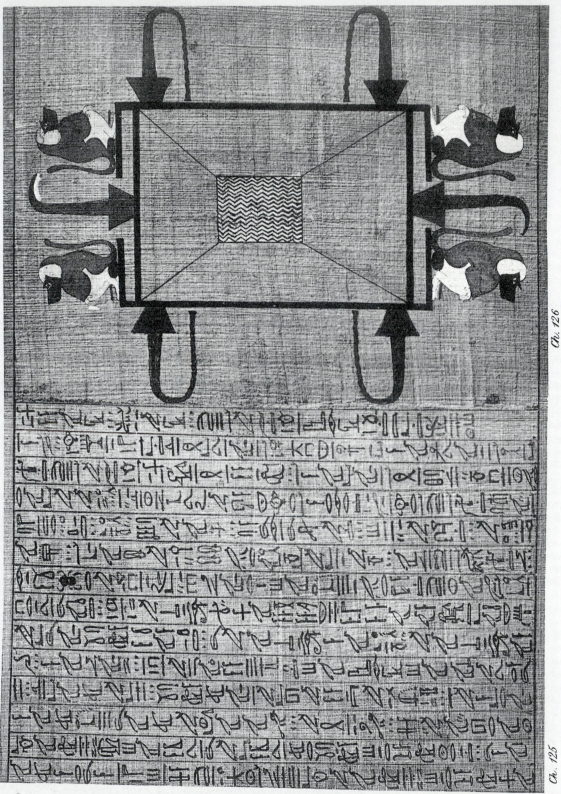

Ch. 126

Ch. 125

PLATE XXIX.

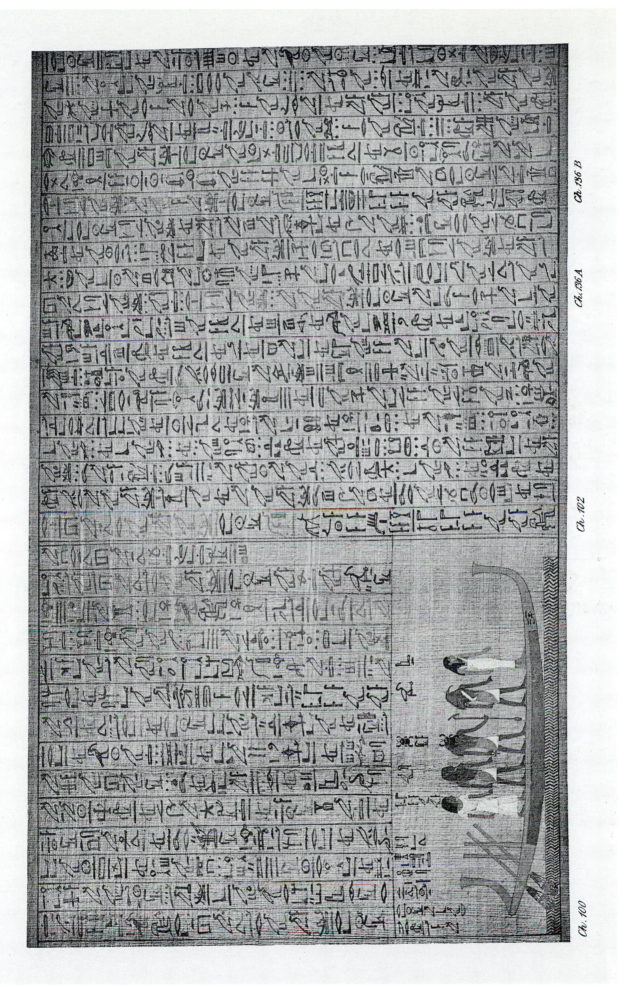

Ch. 102

Ch. 136 A

Ch. 136 B

PLATE XXX

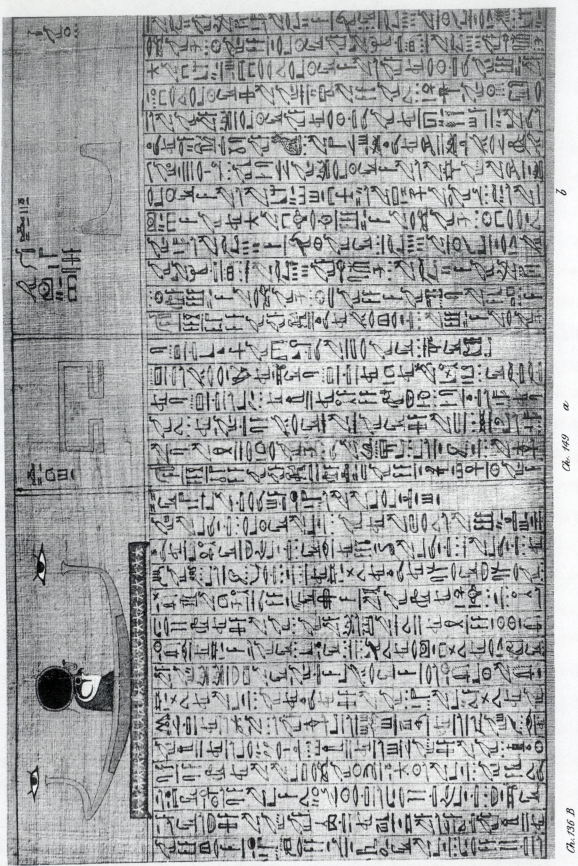

PLATE XXXI.

PLATE XXXI

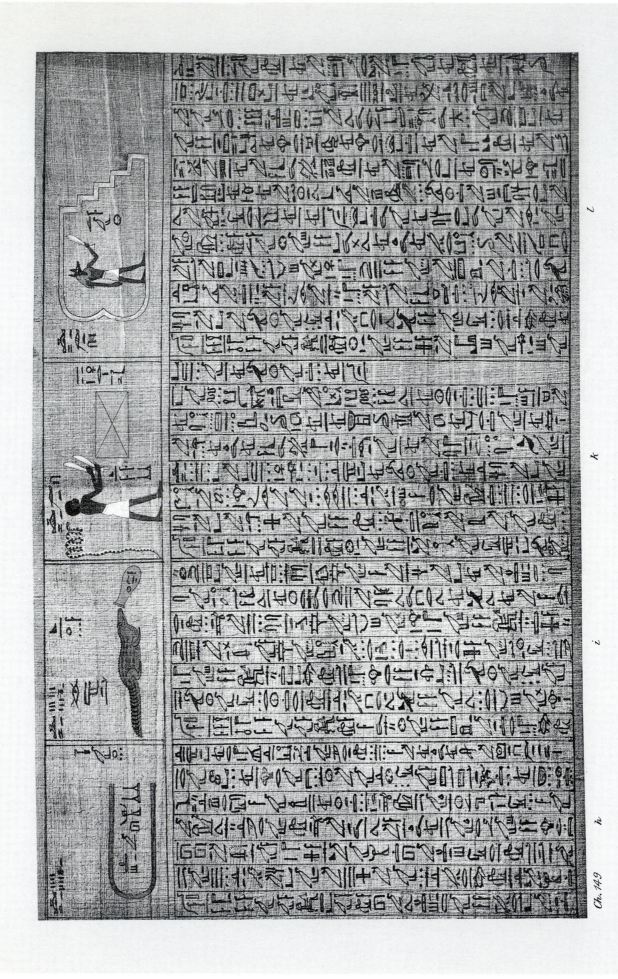

PLATE XXXIII.

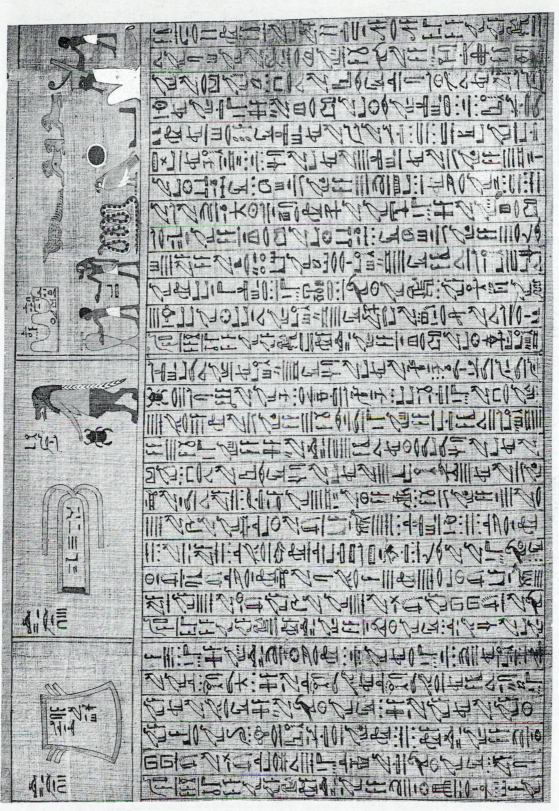

PLATE XXXIV

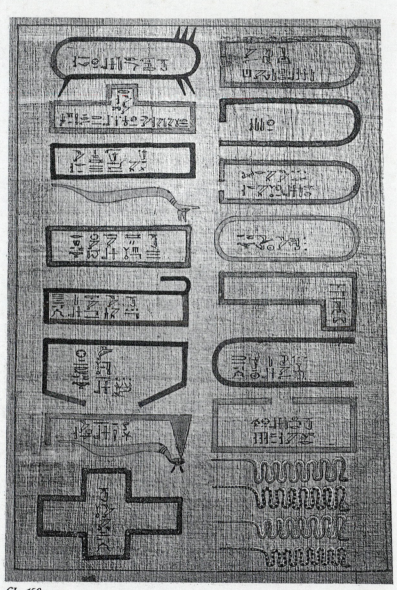

Ch. 150